99% Fat-Free Italian Cooking

Also by Barry Bluestein and Kevin Morrissey

99% Fat-Free Meals in 30 Minutes
The 99% Fat-Free Cookbook
The 99% Fat-Free Book of Appetizers and Desserts
The Complete Cookie
Home Made in the Kitchen
The Bountiful Kitchen
Light Sauces
Quick Breads
Dip It!

Doubleday
New York   London   Toronto   Sydney   Auckland

99% Fat-Free
Italian Cooking

All your favorite dishes

with less than 1 gram of fat

BARRY BLUESTEIN AND KEVIN MORRISSEY

PHOTOGRAPHS BY GRANT KESSLER

PUBLISHED BY DOUBLEDAY
a division of Random House, Inc.
1540 Broadway, New York, New York 10036

DOUBLEDAY and the portrayal of an anchor with a dolphin are trademarks of Doubleday,
a division of Random House, Inc.

Book design by Leah Carlson-Stanisic

Library of Congress Cataloging-in-Publication Data
Bluestein, Barry.
99% fat-free Italian cooking: all your favorite dishes with less than one gram of fat /
Barry Bluestein and Kevin Morrissey.
p.   cm.
Includes index.
1. Low-Fat diet—Recipes.   2. Cookery, Italian.   I. Morrissey, Kevin.   II. Title.
III. Title: Ninety-nine percent fat-ftee Italian cooking.
RM237.7.B583   1999   98-41251
CIP

ISBN 0-385-48545-X

For Claudia Clark Potter—often good,
always lucky, and ever in search of the most scenic sidetrip
even when it's uphill both ways.

Acknowledgments

Special thanks to Jill Van Cleave for her boundless supply of good cheer; to Susan Ramer, our literary agent, for her ongoing encouragement; and to Grant Kessler for his smashing photographs.

As always, we salute our editor, Judy Kern, for her wisdom and wit. We appreciate the help of so many others at Doubleday as well, including Jackie Everly-Warren, Valerie Peterson, Megan Bradley, Theresa Pulle, Skip Dye, and Dorothy Auld.

For their ideas, assistance, and support, we thank Philip Ansalone, Ann Bloomstrand, Eleanor Bluestein, Lisa Ekus, Merrilyn Lewis, William Rice, Martha Schueneman, Mara Tapp, and Mark Sterwald of the Mirro Company.

Last, but hardly least, we would like to acknowledge the inspiration lent by our favorite Italian cooks—baker Nick Malgieri and the first ladies of Italian cuisine, Marcella Hazan, Carol Field, and Lorenza de' Medici.

Contents

99% Fat-Free Italian Cooking

Introduction

A creamy risotto brimming with mussels . . . a bowl of silky fresh spinach pasta dotted with salt cod and tomatoes . . . a skewer of veal threaded around baby spring vegetables . . . an ethereal roasted red pepper flan—such are the rewards of the 99% fat-free Italian kitchen.

Contrary to the misconceptions of Americans reeling from too many overdone pizzas, too many meatballs and sausages, and far, far too much sauce on dishes that would be unfamiliar in Italian homes, Italian cooking and healthful eating are a natural match. Fresh fruits and vegetables, grains, seafood, and minimal saucing are the hallmarks of the real Italian kitchen. Much like health-conscious diners everywhere, Italians have always used meat as an accent rather than as the main component of the meal, have eaten a variety of small courses rather than a huge portion of any single item, and have viewed rich, sugar-laden desserts as special-occasion treats rather than part of the everyday diet.

With the exceptions of tempering the Italian devotion to olive oil and substituting fat-free for full-fat dairy products—but allowing a finishing flourish of heavenly Parmigiano-Reggiano or pecorino cheese, which is well worth the fat grams—little sacrifice is necessary to adapt classic Italian cuisine to a fat-free regimen.

And little is more rewarding. Americans no longer need to be educated about the perils of our traditionally high-fat diet and now understand the role that lowering fat can play in controlling numerous preventable, diet-related health problems. But we nevertheless want real food, thoughtfully conceived and lovingly prepared.

We addressed the issue of paring fat in *The 99% Fat-Free Cookbook* and *The 99% Fat-Free Book of Appetizers and Desserts*. In *99% Fat-Free Meals in 30 Minutes* we demonstrated how to make low-fat cooking quick and easy enough to fit into even the busiest schedule.

The 99% fat-free method is a comprehensive approach to low-fat cooking distinguished by its diner-friendly perspective. By breaking down traditional

recipes and rebuilding them in ways that pare significant amounts of fat at the source, in the kitchen, we provide healthful eating without deprivation. Our simple techniques enable cooks to select ingredients judiciously, to prepare them innovatively, and to dispense with ingrained habits that add superfluous fat.

We now bring this approach to the bountiful Italian table, reducing the fat and indulging guiltlessly in what remains. Although we do need to eschew oil to cook fat-free, we have otherwise tried to be true to Italian flavor combinations, cooking techniques, and dining traditions. We hope you appreciate the Italian way as much as we do. *Buon appetito!*

Suggested Menus

ANTIPASTO MEAL FOR 4

Mussels Casino (page 41)

Eggplant Crostini (page 44)

Tuna Pâté (page 37) with assorted raw vegetables

Stuffed Artichokes (page 164)

Pear and Honey Risotto (page 239)

ANTIPASTO BUFFET FOR 8

Caponata (page 34) and Sardine Paste (page 39; double recipe)
   with Sardinian Flat Bread (page 65)

Veal Spiedini (page 154)

Skewered Lemon Turkey (page 155)

Rapini with Red Pepper (page 186; double recipe)

Orzo Salad with Capers and Tomatoes (page 208)

Campari Sorbet (page 231)

CASUAL BRUNCH

Risotto Cakes (page 79)
   with Yellow Pepper–Mushroom Sauce (page 132)

Roasted Pear and Frisée Salad (page 209)

Lemon Gelato (page 233)

SIMPLE COUNTRY LUNCH

Basil, Bean, and Barley Soup (page 48)

Rustic Italian Bread (page 63)

Arugula Salad with Apple and Bacon (page 200)

Anise Biscotti (page 244)

PICNIC BY THE BEACH

Spicy Chilled Calamari (page 36)

Seafood and Rice Salad with Pesto (page 201)

Sun-Dried Tomato Focaccia (page 218)
Fresh Fruit
Iced Cappuccino

AFTERNOON TEA
Apple Cake (page 240)
Roasted Pears and Blueberries in Balsamic Vinegar (page 230)
Chocolate Raisin Biscotti (page 245)
Assorted Teas

PIZZA PARTY
Individual Roasted Pepper and Portobello Pizzas (page 215)
Eggplant Pizza (page 216)
Vidalia Onion and Poppy Seed Focaccia (page 221)
Sausage Calzones (page 224)
Celeriac Slaw (page 202; double recipe)
Bean and Tomato Salad (page 206; double recipe)

FAMILY DINNER
Tuscan Mussel Stew (page 56)
Soft Breadsticks (page 69)
Rigatoni with Artichokes, Fava Beans, and Arugula (page 104)
Orange-Fennel Salad (page 203)
Amaretto Semifreddo (page 234)

INFORMAL DINNER FOR 4 OR 8
Grilled Calamari and White Bean Salad (page 198; double recipe for 8)
Rapini and Orecchiette (page 96; double recipe for 8)
Fish in Acqua Pazza (page 149; double recipe for 8)
Kale Wilted in Balsamic Vinegar (page 193; double recipe for 8)
Rosemary Bread with Sea Salt Topping (page 64)
Torta di Ricotta (page 241)

DINNER PARTY FOR 4
Parmesan Red Pepper Custard with Tomato Coulis (page 30)
Roasted Tomato Ravioli (page 116) made with Spinach Pasta (page 114)

Chicken Piccata (page 163)
Italian Potatoes with Onion and Rosemary (page 184)
Simmered Greens (page 185)
Chocolate Tiramisù (page 236)
Espresso with Anisette (page 254)

CHAMPAGNE DINNER FOR 6
Roasted Garlic and Onion Soup (page 49)
Quail-Leek Risotto (page 86)
Pork alla Romana (page 165)
Roasted Pepper and Tomato Tart in a Roasted Polenta Shell (page 170)
Green Apple Granita (page 232)
Brut Champagne

DINNER PARTY FOR 8
Broiled Scallops (page 29; double recipe)
Tomato-Fennel Soup (page 55; double recipe)
Grissini (page 66)
Monkfish Osso Buco (page 138; double recipe)
Herb Polenta (page 172)
Fava Bean and Dandelion Green Salad (page 199; double recipe)
Panettone Bread Pudding (page 237)
Assorted Flavored Grappas (pages 250 to 252)

1. The 99% Fat-Free Italian Pantry

Counts, Measurements, and Equivalents

Total fat per serving has been calculated for each recipe to the nearest hundredth of a gram, and total calories to the nearest tenth of a calorie. For commercial ingredients, we use the lowest-fat brands readily available; always compare nutritional labels carefully.

For greater accuracy in calculating fat and calories, most raw ingredients are specified by weight. To help you shop, we generally provide equivalents for weight measurements unless the measured quantity is derived from less than a whole ingredient. For example:

8 ounces plum tomatoes (about 2 tomatoes)
1 pound purple eggplant (about 1 small eggplant)
6 ounces red bell pepper (about 1 pepper)

Cup measurements are provided for most ingredients that are subsequently chopped or diced.

Ingredients

ANCHOVIES: We do use small amounts of anchovies on occasion. They are high in fat, but they impart a distinct flavor that just can't be replicated. Most anchovies come packed in oil, which only adds more fat. Be sure to rinse them thoroughly and pat them dry to blot out any residual oil. If you're able to find anchovies packed in salt, just rinse them lightly. Look for anchovies packed flat and buy the smallest quantity possible, since they tend to become mushy once exposed to the air. (When only a minute amount of anchovy is

needed for a flavor accent, use anchovy paste.) Don't buy the variety wrapped around capers; they are meant as a garnish.

ARUGULA: See Salad Greens, page 14.

BEANS: To soak dried beans, which are always preferable to canned, use 3 cups of water for every 1 cup of beans. (Eight ounces of uncooked beans will produce anywhere from $2\frac{1}{2}$ to $3\frac{1}{2}$ cups of cooked beans. Eight ounces of cannellini beans, the variety we use most often, should yield about $2\frac{1}{2}$ cups cooked.) Cover and let sit for 6 to 8 hours at room temperature. To quick-soak, first bring the water to a boil in a large saucepan. Add the beans, bring back to a boil, and boil for 5 minutes. Cover, remove from the heat, and set aside for 1 hour.

To cook, use 3 cups of fresh water or stock for every 1 cup of soaked beans and cook over high heat until tender, 30 to 60 minutes, depending on the bean. Cannellini beans usually take a good hour. Do not salt the beans before cooking, as this will only toughen their skin. To cook cannellinis in a pressure cooker, combine $3\frac{1}{4}$ cups of water and 1 cup of soaked beans; cook at full pressure, according to the manufacturer's directions, for 9 to 10 minutes.

For vendors of dried beans, see the Source Guide.

If you use canned beans instead of dried, always rinse and drain the beans thoroughly before using them in the recipe. (One #10 can—$14\frac{1}{2}$ to $15\frac{1}{2}$ ounces, depending on the brand—contains about $1\frac{1}{2}$ cups of cooked beans.)

Fresh fava beans are a bit labor-intensive because you must first remove the beans from their pods and then, except when the beans are very young, peel the skin off each one, a task made much easier by blanching the beans after shelling them. To blanch 1 pound of fava beans, bring 4 cups of water to a boil in a medium saucepan over high heat. Add $\frac{1}{4}$ teaspoon of salt and the beans. Cook for 30 seconds, drain, and rinse under cold water. Peel the beans. Favas can be scarce at times; if you can't find them, substitute lima beans.

BEEF STOCK: See page 21.

BLACK PEPPER: Buy whole black peppercorns and grind them as needed. Freshly ground black pepper really is a marked improvement over the pre-ground variety.

BREAD CRUMBS: As all the prepared bread crumbs we know of have a higher fat content than we budget for this ingredient, we make our own by finely grinding dry bread in a food processor or blender. One slice of bread yields 4 to 5 tablespoons of bread crumbs. Use Rustic Italian Bread (page 63) or a commercial product that is low in fat.

CAPERS: Usually, we use small French nonpareil capers only when they are added whole to finish a dish. We use large Italian capers, which have a much stronger flavor, in all other cases. Be sure to rinse off the vinegar in which the capers are bottled before using them.

CHEESE: A very little bit of one of the flavorful Italian hard cheeses typically used to finish pasta dishes goes a long way. It seems a shame to use anything but the best. We constantly use wonderful Parmigiano-Reggiano—the aged, salty Parmesan—as well as the assertive Pecorino Romano, made from sheep's milk, and the softer, creamier Pecorino Toscano. The cheese section of a good supermarket should stock these varieties; also see the Source Guide. Always grate when you are preparing the recipe, and avoid pregrated cheeses.

When ricotta cheese is called for, be sure to use skim-milk ricotta.

For the fat-free mascarpone we use to make tiramisù, see page 24.

CHICKEN STOCK: See page 19.

COCOA POWDER: All our recipes use Dutch processed cocoa powder, which produces a different chemical reaction from other cocoas, which are not treated with an alkali. Compare product labels among Dutch or European-style cocoa powders, which vary in fat content. Use the lowest-fat brand available.

DRIED SEASONING BLEND: See page 22.

EGG SUBSTITUTE AND EGG WHITE: We use both nonfat liquid egg substitute (the kind that can be stored in the freezer and kept far longer than fresh eggs) and egg whites. In many cases they can be used interchangeably; 2 large egg whites equal ¼ cup egg substitute. Read egg substitute labels carefully; be sure to choose a nonfat product and avoid those that contain oil or tofu.

EXTRACTS: Use only pure almond, anise, and vanilla extracts, which are available from most supermarkets or from spice merchants (see the Source Guide).

FENNEL: Choose the kind of fennel that has a round stocky bulb rather than that with a long flat bulb. The former is left longer in the sun and so has a sweeter taste; the elongated variety is bred to ripen quickly.

FLOUR: Several of our bread and pizza recipes call for semolina, the hard durum wheat flour from which dried pasta is made; we also add a little to fresh carrot pasta. We prefer natural unbleached to bleached flour when all-purpose flour is called for, but either will work. Do not, however, make any substitutions for bread flour, which is high in gluten content. Natural and health-food stores usually have a good selection of flours; also see the Source Guide.

GNOCCHI: See pages 118 and 119 for recipes. You can also find acceptable vacuum-packed plain and flavored gnocchi in your supermarket. They're not only convenient but tend to hold their shape better than the store-bought fresh variety, and they taste more like homemade.

HERBS: Since one seldom seems to have enough fresh herbs on hand and because it is so easy to set up a kitchen herb garden, we highly recommend that you grow your own herbs. Many herbs, including basil, oregano, parsley, rosemary, and thyme, do quite well indoors. You won't need a lot of space (a windowsill is ideal), and you can easily augment limited natural light with a grow light. You can start a kitchen herb garden either from seed or from young plants (see the Source Guide). If you start with young plants, or seedlings, you can snip some leaves almost immediately.

Several years ago a friend gave us a little bay plant, which is still flourishing in our sunny kitchen and has now grown to the size of a small tree. It lives indoors year round, like any houseplant, and yields leaves that are remarkably robust and aromatic. Bay leaves can be used to flavor a variety of dishes; some people add a bay leaf to their rice bin as well.

Because we use basil in such quantity, we freeze it prechopped for convenience. Put 6 ounces of basil leaves (about 2 cups) into a food processor along with ¾ cup of boiling water and 2 tablespoons of freshly squeezed lemon juice, which will keep the basil bright green. Process to a fine chop. Pour the mixture into the wells of an ice-cube tray and freeze. When the basil cubes have frozen, pop them out and store them in a plastic freezer bag. Each cube is the equivalent of 2 tablespoons of chopped fresh basil. To flavor sauces and soups, add the cubes intact; for other dishes, thaw and drain first.

To air-dry homegrown herbs, suspend them upside down, out of direct sunlight, for about a week, or dry them in a microwave oven at full power for 3 to 4 minutes. If you substitute dried herbs for fresh, use only about a third as much.

JUICE: Freshly squeezed lemon juice makes a difference and requires virtually no extra effort beyond remembering to keep a supply of lemons on hand. If you substitute commercial orange juice for freshly squeezed, use a variety that is not made from concentrate. To make Carrot Pasta (page 117), extract fresh juice or use frozen organic carrot juice, thawed.

MEAT: We occasionally use small amounts of meat in our fat-free recipes.

Veal scaloppine is a piece of meat from the leanest cut that has been pounded thin. If you want to splurge, you can substitute veal for turkey or chicken breast in many recipes. Veal adds about a fifth of a gram of fat for every ounce used in place of turkey, a tenth of a gram for every ounce used in place of chicken.

For Pork alla Romana (page 165), select thin pieces of lean pork tenderloin.

MILK: We call for skim milk, buttermilk, and evaporated skim milk in our recipes. Contrary to the popular misconception, buttermilk is made from skim milk and contains no butter. Compare the nutrition labels on evaporated skim milks, which can vary in fat content even if they are made by the same manufacturer. Use the lowest-fat variety available.

MUSHROOMS: Since we cannot easily find fresh porcini mushrooms in this country, unfortunately, we must use reconstituted dried porcinis or a mix of dried porcinis and fresh cremini or portobello mushrooms. You may even want to take a crack at growing your own mushrooms, since they can be grown year round under almost any conditions using easy mushroom kits (see the Source Guide).

Drying mushrooms not only extends their shelf life but intensifies their

flavor. Once reconstituted, they do not need to be sautéed, as fresh mushrooms do, before you add them to recipes. You can oven-dry mushrooms for 7 to 8 hours at 170 degrees, leaving the oven door slightly ajar, or dry them in a dehydrator according to the manufacturer's directions.

OIL: Fat-free cooking does not allow for the use of much oil, other than a light spritzing of pans and bowls so that foods won't stick and of ingredients about to go into the oven to facilitate browning. When cooking Italian, we spritz with olive oil, except in sweet baking recipes. Since we use so little, we use the best. Nothing approximates the taste of a high-quality imported olive oil (see the Source Guide). Read labels carefully and select a brand that has been produced *and* bottled in Italy.

Better kitchenware stores now stock a nonaerosol olive oil sprayer that will allow you to dispense a fine mist of olive oil well within our fat count constraints (see the Source Guide). When greasing a cooking surface or bowl, always spread the oil over the surface to coat evenly after spraying.

You can also now obtain commercial cooking spray made from Italian extra-virgin olive oil in better supermarkets.

OLIVES: We use dark brown or black olives that have been salt-cured and packed in brine, not oil, and actually prefer the slightly stronger taste of kalamata olives to that of the milder Italian varieties. To pit olives easily, push down with the side of a chef's knife to flatten the olive and split it open.

PASTA: During the past year or two, several brands of dried pasta that are low in fat have come onto the market, including some high-quality imports from Italy (see the Source Guide). Not only are the imports considerably more flavorful than the domestic brands, but they often contain only about half the fat of the typical American brand. Look for a product that has no more than half a gram of fat for every 2 ounces.

We prefer fresh pasta made at home to the commercial variety, which is almost always made with fatty egg yolk anyway. Homemade Pasta (page 111) not only tastes better but is virtually fat-free, since we make it with an egg white-based egg substitute. We also make Carrot Pasta (page 117) and Spinach Pasta (page 114). All three pastas can be cut into strands or stuffed.

PASTES: Choose tomato paste and sun-dried tomato paste imported from Italy in tubes (see the Source Guide). Look for a "double concentrate" for stronger flavor, and be sure to select a brand made without olive oil or preservatives.

A high-quality sun-dried tomato paste can be mixed with water for a delicious, quick sauce. Use 2 to 3 tablespoons of water for every 1 tablespoon of paste.

POLENTA: We use several different types of cornmeal for this versatile dish, including white and yellow cornmeals, fine-ground domestic cornmeal, and the coarse-ground Italian cornmeal most often imported to the United States, which is sometimes labeled "polenta" (see the Source Guide). You can also mix cornmeals of various textures or colors to achieve a desired consistency or hue.

POULTRY: We use lean cuts of turkey and chicken, which are quite low in fat when properly trimmed. Keep a few simple guidelines in mind when shopping.

⌒ When ground poultry is called for, avoid preground meat, which can contain a considerable amount of hidden fat. Each recipe includes directions for doing your own grinding. Alternatively, you can select a lean cut and have your butcher trim and grind the meat.

⌒ Turkey breast tenderloin, the leanest part of the breast, is readily available prepackaged.

⌒ Buy skinless, boneless chicken breasts trimmed of all visible fat, preferably from the butcher. (You only need to look closely at some of the prepackaged commercial brands laden with gobs of fat to know what we mean.) A little chicken goes a long way; it's worth the splurge to buy Amish or other free-range products.

RICE: Although you can use readily available Arborio rice for risotto, our first choice would be Vialone Nano rice, which produces the creamiest risottos we've ever had. A close second choice would be Carnaroli rice. Neither can be found in most supermarkets, but they are well worth ordering specially (see the Source Guide). An interesting recent discovery is Cal Riso,

a cross between Italian and Californian rice varieties that closely resembles the Carnaroli strain (also see the Source Guide).

ROASTED GARLIC: In addition to roasting your own garlic (see page 23), you can now buy a brand of preroasted, vacuum-packed cloves; look in the fresh pasta refrigerator case of better supermarkets. In a pinch, use the minced roasted garlic sold in jars in supermarket produce aisles, which is less acidic than plain chopped garlic packaged this way.

ROASTED PEPPERS: For convenience we sometimes use commercially prepared roasted bell peppers, found in jars with the Italian goods in most markets. You can now buy both red and yellow roasted sweet peppers.

To roast your own peppers, preheat the broiler and line the rack with aluminum foil. Cut the peppers in half lengthwise and core and seed them. Place them on the rack cut side down, 2 to 3 inches from the heat source. Broil for about 5 minutes, until they are charred. Carefully transfer them to an airtight plastic bag and let them cool for about 10 minutes, after which the skin should rub off easily. These can be stored in the refrigerator for up to 5 days or frozen in heavy-duty plastic freezer bags for up to 1 month.

Bell peppers lose about a third of their weight when cored, seeded, roasted, and peeled, so start with 9 ounces of bell pepper to get 6 ounces of roasted pepper.

SALAD GREENS: It has become so frustrating trying to find arugula and radicchio at times that we've taken to growing our own, along with frisée and an assortment of other salad greens. This is not a particularly difficult task, as evidenced by the fact that we do it on the window ledge of our nineteenth-floor apartment. We happen to have a sunny exposure, but if you don't, you can easily help things along with a grow light. Start your lettuce crop from seeds (see the Source Guide); they can easily keep you in fresh greens for 2 to 4 months.

Look for French rather than Italian arugula. The Italian variety is hard to find in the United States, and the readily available French arugula can be grown easily in a pot on the windowsill.

SALT: When we call for coarse salt in recipes, our salt of choice is kosher salt, which is readily available in most supermarkets and has less sodium per measure than finer-grained table salt. Otherwise we use sea salt, which we grind from coarse crystals to a fine consistency. You can find coarse sea-salt crystals in better supermarkets; also see the Source Guide.

SEAFOOD: Seafood is a staple in our kitchen. It's low in fat, quick to prepare, full of flavor, and adds just the needed touch of panache to a quick and healthful entertaining menu.

⌐ When blue mussels are called for in a recipe, look for debearded mussels for convenience; they're usually packaged in mesh bags. Rinse the mussels under cold running water, scrubbing the shells lightly if necessary to dislodge residual sand and discarding those that don't close when tapped and those that have broken shells. The mussels should open naturally while cooking; discard any that don't. Some recipes call for green-lip mussels from New Zealand, which admittedly are not authentically Italian but are a real boon to the harried cook. They come partially cooked and frozen on the half shell (always thaw them before using). They are considerably larger than blue mussels and can make for an attractive presentation.

⌐ We usually choose bay scallops rather than the larger sea scallops when they are available. Be aware that a certain gamble is involved. Sea scallops are consistently good. Bay scallops vary in quality but can't be equaled when they're in their prime. If you are substituting an equal weight of sea scallops for bay scallops, quarter them before cooking.

⌐ Use readily available cleaned squid, fresh or frozen, for convenience. Almost all squid sold in the United States arrives frozen from Asia or the Mediterranean. The only difference between the prepackaged squid in the seafood freezer case and that sold at the fish counter is that you won't need to defrost the latter. There should no discernible odor as squid thaws. Look for baby octopus for the Baby Octopus Ragù (page 140) in Italian, Greek, or Asian markets, which usually stock it trimmed and cleaned; substitute small squid if you can't find it.

⌐ We prefer littleneck clams to larger varieties—they're sweeter, less likely to toughen when cooked, and make for a very abundant plate when served up in the shell. Remember that clams are alive until cooked, which necessitates a few extra precautionary steps. If you buy clams prepackaged in a plastic-wrapped Styrofoam container, punch a few holes in the

plastic before you put the container in the refrigerator to allow the clams to breathe. Rinse the clams thoroughly, as you would mussels, discarding those that don't close when tapped and any with broken shells. The clams should open naturally while cooking; discard any that don't.

⁓ Unless a specific recipe calls for cooked shrimp, use raw shrimp so as not to overcook and toughen the shrimp.

⁓ We use extremely low-fat cod liberally. We also make use of various other white fish, including tilapia, a relative newcomer that is farm-raised, extremely low in fat, and easily filleted.

SUN-DRIED TOMATOES: Sun-dried tomatoes can be purchased prepared (red or yellow tomatoes halved, red tomatoes chopped), or you can dry tomatoes at home.

To dry your own tomatoes, preheat the oven to 170 degrees. Cut Italian plum tomatoes in half lengthwise and place them on a cookie sheet, cut side up. Bake for at least 6 hours (the time needed can vary quite a bit), until the tomatoes are dry, deep reddish brown, and still somewhat elastic. Do not allow them to blacken or become brittle. Let them cool completely and store in airtight containers.

TOMATOES: Although we use fresh tomatoes when they are in season, many of our recipes allow for the use of boxed or canned tomatoes the rest of the year. (They are actually preferable to hothouse tomatoes, since they are allowed to ripen longer on the vine and have been peeled and seeded.) Our favorite products are Pomì brand, imported from Italy. Packaged in boxes, they consist of pure chopped or strained tomatoes with no additives. (Pomì also makes a marinara sauce.) When selecting imported canned tomatoes, look for the San Marzano variety.

To peel and seed fresh tomatoes, cut an *X* into the bloom end of each and submerge them in a pot of boiling water. Cook for 2 to 3 minutes, until the tomatoes rise to the top. Rinse them briefly under cold running water and peel back the skin from the split that will have opened at each *X*. Quarter the tomatoes and remove the seeds.

VEGETABLE STOCK: See page 20.

VINEGAR: We make liberal use of balsamic vinegar, which, though indulgent, is sweeter than other vinegars, especially in our oil-free salad dressings. The best varieties of *balsamico* are aged for years in a succession of wooden casks. See the Source Guide for vendors.

YEAST: Recipes are formulated for the use of active dry yeast, not quick-rising yeast.

Equipment

(See the Source Guide for vendors.)

FOOD PROCESSOR: It's hard to cook these days without a food processor, which pares many meal preparation chores to a fraction of the time they would otherwise require. In some cases a blender can be substituted, especially when you are working with a more liquid mixture and when you want a very smooth consistency.

MOLDS: Although you can make panettone in a soufflé mold or in a coffee can, which will approximate the traditional shape, the prettiest panettones by far emerge from specially designed (and relatively inexpensive) molds. Brioche molds are similar in shape to panettone molds and add a little more flair to individual servings of Panettone Bread Pudding (page 237) than do ramekins.

PASTA-MAKING EQUIPMENT: A pasta machine, especially an inexpensive crank model, is well worth the investment and can be augmented with a variety of attachments for making shaped pastas. (We avoid pasta extruders, for which our fresh doughs tend to be a little too delicate.) An equally wise investment is a pasta drying rack, on which you can easily dry strands of fresh pasta with little disruption to your kitchen. Ravioli molds make quick work of shaped pastas (use perogi molds for agnolotti).

A pot with a pasta insert makes it a lot easier to drain and toss just-cooked pasta quickly; a pasta fork also facilitates removing cooked pasta from the water easily.

PRESSURE COOKER: We've recently rediscovered the pressure cooker, which can considerably cut down the time involved in preparing long-cooking stews, beans, and stocks. The new lines of pressure cookers are particularly suited to quick preparation of fat-free meals, since they don't require the addition of oil or other superfluous fats. One manufacturer has even introduced a model especially designed for making risottos.

SKILLETS AND SAUCEPANS: We often use nonstick skillets, which eliminate the need for oil—preferably heavy-bottomed skillets that will heat evenly and won't warp over high heat. Do not, however, use nonstick pans to make polenta. One of your primary "doneness" cues is that the cornmeal mixture pulls away from the sides of the pan easily when stirred, which it will do from the start in a nonstick pan.

We're particularly fond of skillets and saucepans with glass lids, which allow you to monitor cooking without removing the lids.

Chicken Stock

4 pounds chicken bones, with a few
  scraps of meat left on
3 carrots (unpeeled), trimmed and cut
  into chunks
2 parsnips (unpeeled), trimmed and
  quartered lengthwise
1 large yellow onion, cut into 1-inch
  chunks

5 stalks celery, trimmed and quartered
15 sprigs flat-leaf parsley, ends
  trimmed
Water to cover above ingredients by 2
  inches (about 5 quarts)
12 whole black peppercorns

Put the chicken bones, vegetables, and parsley in a large stockpot. Cover with water. Bring to a rapid boil over high heat, then skim the foamy residue off the top. Reduce the heat to low and simmer, uncovered, for about 4 hours, until the bones begin to disintegrate. Periodically skim the residue off the top.

Remove the pot from the heat. Discard all solid ingredients from the stock and strain the liquid into a large bowl. Add the peppercorns. Refrigerate, uncovered, for at least 2 to 3 hours. If refrigerating overnight, cover after 2 to 3 hours.

When you take the stock out of the refrigerator, use a large spoon to lift off as much as possible of the layer of fat that has settled on top. Using a dinner knife, scrape along the top of the stock to catch any additional small pieces of fat.

For a clearer stock, put it into a large pot and cook over medium heat for 2 to 3 minutes, until it has turned from a gelatinous state back into liquid. Pour the liquefied stock through a strainer lined with a double layer of cheesecloth (to strain sediment and peppercorns) into a clean bowl.

Yield = 6 to 8 cups

Once the fat has been skimmed, good old-fashioned chicken stock is a fat-free cook's best friend! We recommend making your own in order to control the taste and fat content. It will keep for up to 3 days in the refrigerator and can be frozen in handy 2-cup portions in heavy-duty plastic freezer bags to have on hand for quick meal preparation.

By using a pressure cooker, you can cut down the cooking time for the stock to about 40 minutes and eliminate the need to skim while cooking. To make this volume of stock, use at least an 8-quart cooker, filled no more than two-thirds full, and follow the manufacturer's directions.

If you use commercial chicken stock rather than making your own, refrigerate, skim, and strain it according to the directions at left before proceeding to use the stock in a recipe.

Vegetable Stock

FLAVORFUL HOMEMADE vegetable stock is always preferable to canned when you have a bit of extra time to make a batch of your own. It will keep for up to 3 days in the refrigerator and can be frozen in 2-cup portions in heavy-duty plastic freezer bags. You can speed up the cooking time to about 30 minutes by using a pressure cooker; see directions in the recipe for Chicken Stock on page 19.

When choosing commercial stock, compare nutrition labels, as some brands include ingredients that add fat to the stock. Choose the lowest-fat variety available.

1 large yellow onion, coarsely chopped

2 medium leeks, trimmed, rinsed, and sliced

2 tomatoes (or 6 plum tomatoes), coarsely chopped

4 carrots, peeled and coarsely chopped

4 cloves garlic, peeled

3 stalks celery, trimmed and sliced

10 sprigs flat-leaf parsley, ends trimmed

6 whole black peppercorns

4 bay leaves

4 quarts water

Combine all the ingredients in a large stockpot. Bring to a boil over medium-high heat. Reduce the heat to low and simmer gently, uncovered, for 2 hours.

Strain into a large bowl, pressing down on the vegetables to extract as much liquid as possible.

Yield = 6 to 8 cups

Beef Stock

3 pounds beef bones, with a few
  scraps of meat left on
1 large yellow onion, peeled, peels
  reserved
1 tomato, quartered, or 3 plum
  tomatoes, halved

2 carrots (unpeeled), trimmed and
  halved
2 stalks celery, trimmed and halved
4 bay leaves
5 quarts water

Preheat the oven to 450 degrees. Line a baking pan that is just large enough to hold the bones in a single layer with aluminum foil. Place the beef bones in the pan. Roast for about 30 minutes, until the bones are very brown, turning once after 15 minutes. Transfer the bones to paper towels, which will absorb any residual fat.

Meanwhile, put the vegetables in a second pan and roast for 20 minutes, turning once after 10 minutes.

Combine the roasted beef bones and vegetables, the reserved onion peels, and the bay leaves in a large stockpot. Cover with the water. Bring to a rapid boil over high heat and skim off the foamy residue that rises to the top. Turn the heat down to low and simmer, uncovered, for about 4 hours, skimming periodically.

Remove the pot from the heat and discard all the solid ingredients. Be sure to remove the bay leaves. Strain the liquid into a large bowl and refrigerate, uncovered, for at least 2 to 3 hours. If refrigerating overnight, cover after 2 to 3 hours.

Remove the stock from the refrigerator and use a large spoon to lift off the layer of fat that has settled over the top. Then scrape along the top with a dinner knife to catch any small pieces of fat that remain.

For a clearer stock, return it to a large pot and cook over medium heat for 2 to 3 minutes, until liquefied. Pour the liquefied stock through a strainer lined with a double layer of cheesecloth into a clean bowl.

Yield = 6 to 8 cups

ROASTING THE BEEF bones and vegetables for this stock yields a much deeper color and a richer taste than you'll ever find in a commercial stock, and homemade stock contains a considerably lower amount of sodium. To make the stock in an 8-quart pressure cooker, fill the cooker no more than two-thirds full and follow the manufacturer's directions; the cooking time should be reduced to about 45 minutes.

Beef Stock will keep for up to 3 days in the refrigerator and can be frozen in 2-cup portions in heavy-duty plastic freezer bags.

If you use a commercial stock, be sure to choose a fat-free (preskimmed) variety.

Dried Seasoning Blend

THIS HOMEMADE seasoning mixture is far more aromatic than most commercial blends. It's great on salads, poultry, and seafood. Remember to store seasonings in opaque containers, in which they will remain fresh and flavorful for 6 months to 1 year.

2 tablespoons dried thyme

2 tablespoons dried oregano

2 tablespoons dried rosemary

1 tablespoon dried marjoram

1 teaspoon dried winter savory

1 teaspoon ground sage

1 teaspoon dried basil

Mix all ingredients together well.

Yield = ¹/₂ cup

 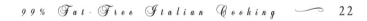

Roasted Garlic

One 3½- to 4-ounce head garlic
½ cup Chicken Stock (page 19)

Preheat the oven to 350 degrees.

Slice off about ¼ inch of the stem end of the garlic, exposing the tips of the cloves. Place the whole head in an 8-ounce ramekin and add the stock. (The stock should come about halfway up the sides of the garlic.) Cover with aluminum foil and bake for about 1 hour, until a knife can be inserted easily into the top of the head.

Yield = 1 head roasted garlic

UTTER SIMPLICITY, yet somehow inexplicably botched by many a restaurant in the United States. Perhaps there's an object lesson here: in restaurants, order the tricky, time-consuming concoctions best left to chefs; savor the heady sensation of aromatic garlic fresh from the oven and smeared on equally robust bread at home, in your own kitchen.

In addition to using roasted garlic in cooking, we serve it surrounded by slices of Anise Bread (page 68) or other savory breads.

To roast loose cloves, peel them, wrap them in aluminum foil, and bake for only 15 to 20 minutes.

Mascarpone

OUR FAT-FREE rendition has none of the fat but much of the rich flavor of mascarpone cheese. In addition to using it in Chocolate Tiramisù (page 236), you could dollop some on our Apple Cake (page 240) or on fresh fruit.

1 cup plain nonfat yogurt	2 tablespoons buttermilk

Line a strainer with a coffee filter and suspend it over a glass or ceramic bowl. Empty the yogurt into the strainer and place the bowl in the refrigerator to chill and drain for 3 to 4 hours.

Remove the yogurt cheese that remains in the strainer to a mixing bowl and stir in the buttermilk. Cover with plastic wrap and set aside at room temperature for 6 hours.

Mascarpone will keep for several days in the refrigerator.

Yield = About ⅔ cup

Appetizers

(Antipasti)

Broiled Scallops ⟶ Parmesan–Red Pepper Custard with Tomato Coulis ⟶ Artichoke Flan in Lemon Broth ⟶ Caponata ⟶ Spicy Chilled Calamari ⟶ Tuna Pâté ⟶ White Bean Spread ⟶ Sardine Paste ⟶ Stuffed Eggplant ⟶ Mussels Casino ⟶ Roasted Peppers with Anchovy Sauce on Polenta Crostini ⟶ Eggplant Crostini

2. *Appetizers*

(Antipasti)

Many of us who can remember back to mid-century America thought at the time that we knew perfectly well what an antipasto was—a plate piled with sliced salami (usually only a single variety), cubes of soft white cheese of indeterminate origin, and lots of pickled hot peppers. It was the course that preceded the platter of oversauced spaghetti in the dining room of the local pizza parlor.

By the 1970s, the world had shrunk and the American palate had broadened enough that we had learned to serve pastas in their proper place—as *primi,* first courses—and had grown to appreciate a variety of poultry, seafood, and meat entrees, or *secondi.* But it wasn't until years later, usually after traveling in Italy, that most of us came to savor the seemingly endless range of antipasti that lie beyond that humble plate of salami and cheese— or, indeed, to realize how much more sophisticated and satisfying a simple arrangement of cold meat and cheese could be.

Much like Americans, Italians are eating lighter today. What would once have been the start of a lavish meal may now be the meal itself. One is more likely to see a formal dinner that starts with antipasti in a restaurant than at home. And even in the gastronomically indulgent Piedmont region, meals are no longer routinely initiated with 10 or 12 antipasti.

Antipasti, however, are not on the wane. Beguiling yet rather innocent at heart, they're well suited to the way we eat today. As an appetizer or on a buffet, served singly for a light lunch or supper or grouped to compose an engaging dinner, antipasti charm and satisfy without overwhelming.

As our sampling shows, antipasti run the gamut from ethereal flans to earthy stuffed vegetables, from chilled calamari flecked with bell pepper and capers to bubbly, crusty scallops topped with parsley and bread crumbs, hot from the broiler.

Our methods of paring fat from these dishes are as varied as the antipasti themselves. We focus on fresh vegetables and low-fat seafood. We may

replace bread with a slice of eggplant as a crostini base, use an egg substitute made from egg whites in lieu of whole eggs in a custard, or strip anchovies of the oil in which they were packed. But if an antipasto begs to be topped with a grating of fresh cheese, it will always be Parmigiano-Reggiano!

Broiled Scallops

¼ cup bread crumbs (see Pantry)
1 tablespoon chopped fresh flat-leaf
 parsley
1 teaspoon paprika

½ teaspoon grated lemon zest
Olive oil cooking spray
8 ounces bay scallops

Preheat the broiler.

In a bowl, combine the bread crumbs, parsley, paprika, and lemon zest. Mix well.

Spray four 2- to 3-ounce gratin dishes or ramekins lightly with olive oil and place them on a baking sheet. Put ¼ cup scallops in each ramekin and top with 4 teaspoons of the bread crumb mixture. Broil until the topping is well browned and steaming and the scallops are firm to the touch and opaque, about 5 minutes.

Yield = 4 servings
Fat per serving = 0.55 g.
Calories per serving = 59.5

IN THIS RECIPE, WE adapt a traditional Adriatic-style preparation for grilled shrimp to scallops. The scallops are coated ever so lightly with oil, covered in a seasoned parsley and bread crumb mixture, and broiled. Serving the dish in scallop shells instead of gratin dishes or ramekins adds a stylish touch for dinner parties.

Parmesan-Red Pepper Custard with Tomato Coulis

Olive oil cooking spray

7 ounces roasted sweet red pepper (see Pantry)

1 tablespoon plus 1 teaspoon all-purpose flour

½ cup buttermilk

½ cup nonfat liquid egg substitute (see Pantry)

½ teaspoon sugar

Salt and freshly ground black pepper to taste

2 tablespoons freshly grated Parmigiano-Reggiano cheese

2 to 3 cups boiling water

2 tablespoons tomato paste

2 tablespoons Sambuca liqueur

1 tablespoon small capers (nonpareils), drained

2 dashes hot sauce

1 teaspoon chopped fresh oregano

Preheat the oven to 375 degrees. Spray each of four 4-ounce ramekins lightly with olive oil and spread the oil over the surface to coat.

Put the roasted pepper into the bowl of a food processor or blender and puree until smooth.

Combine the flour and buttermilk in a medium saucepan over medium heat. Whisking constantly, cook for about 3 minutes, until the mixture is just beginning to steam. Remove from the heat. Whisk in ½ cup of the roasted pepper puree (reserving 2 tablespoons for the sauce), the egg substitute, sugar, salt, black pepper, and Parmesan. Divide the mixture among the prepared ramekins, set them into a baking dish, and fill the dish halfway up the sides of the ramekins with boiling water. Bake for about 35 minutes, until firm.

For the sauce, combine the tomato paste, Sambuca, capers, hot sauce, oregano, and the remaining 2 tablespoons roasted red pepper puree in a food processor or blender and process until smooth.

Remove the custards from the oven and let them sit for 5 minutes. Unmold each one onto a small plate by placing the plate over the ramekin, inverting both, and shaking the mold to dislodge the custard. Spoon about 1 table-spoon of sauce around each custard.

Yield = 4 servings
Fat per serving = 0.73 g.
Calories per serving = 77.1

individual custards are served floating in a lemony chicken broth and garnished with sprigs of parsley. If your market is out of frozen artichoke hearts, look for a supply at the salad bar. You can easily roast your own garlic from scratch. In a pinch, use preroasted garlic. It's now available vacuum-packed—look in the refrigerator case with fresh pastas—as well as in jars in the produce department (see Pantry).

Artichoke Flan in Lemon Broth

Olive oil cooking spray

One 9-ounce package frozen artichoke hearts, thawed, excess water squeezed out

1 teaspoon minced roasted garlic

¾ cup nonfat liquid egg substitute (see Pantry)

½ cup buttermilk

1½ tablespoons all-purpose flour

⅛ teaspoon ground white pepper

Salt to taste

2 to 3 cups boiling water

1 cup Chicken Stock (see page 19)

Zest of 1 lemon

1 tablespoon freshly squeezed lemon juice

1 tablespoon chopped fresh flat-leaf parsley plus 4 whole sprigs for garnish

Preheat the oven to 375 degrees. Coat four 4-ounce ramekins lightly with the olive oil cooking spray.

In the bowl of a food processor or blender, combine the artichoke hearts, garlic, ½ cup of the liquid egg substitute, and ¼ cup of the buttermilk. Puree for 1 to 2 minutes, until smooth.

In a small saucepan, combine the remaining ¼ cup buttermilk and the flour. Stir until smooth and cook over medium heat for a minute or two, stirring constantly, until the mixture is steaming. Stir in the artichoke puree, white pepper, and salt. Divide among the prepared ramekins, place them in a baking dish filled with boiling water to come halfway up the sides of the ramekins, and bake for about 30 minutes, until a tester inserted into the center of a custard comes out clean. Remove the ramekins to a wire rack and allow them to cool for 5 minutes.

Meanwhile, for the sauce, combine the Chicken Stock and the remaining ¼ cup egg substitute in a small saucepan over medium heat. Cook for 2 minutes, then add the lemon zest, lemon juice, and chopped parsley. Stirring constantly, continue to cook for about 3 minutes, until the sauce is steaming vigorously.

Ladle about ⅓ cup sauce into each of 4 pasta bowls. Gently unmold a flan into the center of each and garnish with a sprig of parsley.

Yield = 4 servings
Fat per serving = 0.39 g.
Calories per serving = 71.8

CAPONATA IS A TASTY eggplant-based vegetable mix perfect for a buffet, since it's best served at room temperature. Our rendition is a shade less sweet than traditional Sicilian caponatas, since we don't add sugar, but we also replace the usual olives with a bit of roasted sweet red pepper. Originally caponata was served on sea biscuits, as a somewhat more elaborate Genoese version still is, but we like ours with Sardinian Flat Bread (page 65).

Caponata

1 pound purple eggplant (about 1 small eggplant)
1 pound plum tomatoes (4 to 5 tomatoes)
1 tablespoon coarse salt
Olive oil cooking spray
4 ounces scallions (about 8 scallions), trimmed to white and light green parts and cut into chunks
4 cloves garlic, peeled

7 ounces roasted sweet red pepper (see Pantry)
2 tablespoons fresh flat-leaf parsley
2 teaspoons fresh thyme leaves
2 tablespoons capers, drained
1 tablespoon freshly squeezed lemon juice
$\frac{1}{8}$ teaspoon freshly ground black pepper
$\frac{1}{2}$ cup balsamic vinegar

Peel the eggplant and cut it into $\frac{1}{2}$-inch cubes. Cut the tomatoes in half lengthwise.

Put the eggplant cubes into a colander, sprinkle with 2 teaspoons of the salt, toss, and place in the sink to drain for about 30 minutes.

Preheat the oven to 350 degrees. Line a baking sheet with aluminum foil.

Toss the eggplant and let it drain for 30 minutes more. While the eggplant drains, lay the tomatoes cut side up on a rack on the prepared baking sheet. Sprinkle with the remaining teaspoon salt and bake for 30 minutes.

Turn the tomatoes over and bake for another 30 minutes. Meanwhile, rinse the eggplant under cold water for 1 minute, then wrap it in a towel and squeeze out as much moisture as possible. Lightly spray a second baking sheet with olive oil, lay the eggplant on the sheet in a single layer, and bake for 15 minutes. Toss and bake for about 15 minutes more, until just beginning to brown.

Combine the eggplant, tomatoes, scallions, garlic, roasted red pepper, parsley, thyme, capers, lemon juice, and black pepper in the bowl of a food processor. Pulse about 15 times to form a course puree. Transfer to a serving bowl and stir in the vinegar.

Yield = About 2 cups, or 32 tablespoons
Fat per tablespoon = 0.07 g.
Calories per tablespoon = 8.1

Spicy Chilled Calamari

CALAMARI—WONDERFUL in so many ways, from salads to stews to simple grilled preparations—have gone mainstream in much of the United States in recent years, but Kevin still remembers the inquisitive stares that often accompanied a plateful served in a Chicago restaurant back in the 1960s.

This antipasto is rather like a squid salad without the greens. It's simple to prepare (just blanch, dress, and chill) and light enough to be served with a sampling of complimentary antipasti. Use the diminutive nonpareil capers, since they're added whole.

8 ounces cleaned squid with tentacles (see Pantry)
1/4 cup freshly squeezed lemon juice
10 drops hot sauce
2 tablespoons chopped fresh flat-leaf parsley
1 tablespoon small capers (nonpareils), drained
1/4 cup diced red bell pepper
2 cloves garlic, chopped
1/2 teaspoon chopped fresh oregano
Salt to taste

Cut the squid bodies into 1/2-inch rings. You should have about 1 cup rings and tentacles combined.

Fill a medium saucepan three-quarters full of water and bring to a boil. Add the squid and cook over medium-high heat for about 45 seconds, until opaque and firm. Drain and transfer to a bowl. Add the lemon juice, hot sauce, parsley, capers, bell pepper, garlic, oregano, and salt. Mix thoroughly. Cover and refrigerate for at least 1 hour before serving.

Serve a generous 1/4 cup to each person.

Yield = 6 servings
Fat per serving = 0.19 g.
Calories per serving = 26.2

Tuna Pâté

One 6-ounce can albacore tuna
  packed in water, drained
1 tablespoon capers, drained
2 tablespoons freshly squeezed lemon
  juice
1 teaspoon anchovy paste

1 teaspoon minced roasted garlic (see
  Pantry)
2 tablespoons skim-milk ricotta cheese

Combine the tuna, capers, lemon juice, anchovy paste, garlic, and ricotta in the bowl of a food processor or blender and puree until smooth.

Yield = About ¾ cup, or 12 tablespoons
Fat per tablespoon = 0.18 g.
Calories per tablespoon = 19.0

PÂTÉS ARE particularly popular in the northwestern part of Italy, reflecting the region's proximity to France. You can't find an antipasto much simpler than this preparation—and the results are pleasant indeed. Be sure to use freshly squeezed lemon juice and to choose the best-quality albacore tuna you can find. Some cooks swear by brands of tuna imported from Italy, but we've yet to find one packed in water instead of fatty oil. We usually stuff celery with the pâté, but it would also be good on bread, crackers, or crostini.

White Bean Spread

THIS SPREAD FEATURES cannellinis, the white beans so popular in all regions of Italy, flavored with fresh herbs, lemon, garlic, and balsamic vinegar. The bits of sun-dried tomato folded in add color and a bit of textural contrast as well. Serve on slices of Italian bread, toasted and cut into thirds.

If you use canned rather than dried beans, be sure to rinse and drain them thoroughly.

1½ cups cooked cannellini beans (see Pantry)
2 tablespoons fresh flat-leaf parsley
1 tablespoon chopped fresh rosemary
2 tablespoons freshly squeezed lemon juice
2 tablespoons balsamic vinegar
2 cloves garlic, peeled
4 sun-dried tomatoes
¼ cup water
Freshly ground black pepper to taste

Combine the beans, parsley, rosemary, lemon juice, and vinegar in a food processor or blender. Press in the garlic. Puree until smooth and transfer the spread to a bowl.

Combine the sun-dried tomatoes and water in a small microwave-safe bowl and microwave at full power for about 1½ minutes, until the tomatoes are soft. Remove the tomatoes from the water and chop fine. (You should have a generous tablespoon.) Fold into the bean spread and add pepper to taste.

Yield = About 1 cup, or 16 tablespoons
Fat per tablespoon = 0.20 g.
Calories per tablespoon = 21.0

Sardine Paste

One 5½-ounce can sardines in tomato
  sauce with chili
1 tablespoon freshly squeezed lemon
  juice
2 tablespoons nonfat sour cream
1 teaspoon minced roasted garlic (see
  Pantry)

6 drops hot sauce
1 tablespoon chopped fresh basil
½ tablespoon chopped fresh flat-leaf
  parsley
½ teaspoon prepared white
  horseradish
Salt to taste

Drain the sardines and remove any large bones. Put them into the bowl of
a food processor and pulse twice. Add the lemon juice, sour cream, garlic,
hot sauce, basil, parsley, horseradish, and salt. Process until smooth. Cover
and chill for at least 2 hours before serving.

Yield = About 9 tablespoons
Fat per tablespoon = 0.35 g.
Calories per tablespoon = 20.9

WE LIKE SARDINES almost as much as Sicilians do, and we keep coming up with new ways to use them. With roasted garlic, hot sauce, and horseradish, this particular concoction is not for those with timid palates. It's particularly good with both Grissini (page 66) and Sardinian Flat Bread (page 65).

We start with sardines in tomato sauce seasoned with chili pepper. We've found several brands of sardines packed this way. If your market doesn't stock any, buy the variety in plain tomato sauce and add a little chopped hot chili pepper.

Stuffed Eggplant

These eggplant boats are filled with a seasoned mixture of tomato, zucchini, diced eggplant, and rice. We pass by more exotic offerings in favor of the readily available purple eggplant, which is similar to the Black Beauty variety found in Italy. (Seeds for Black Beauty eggplant are now available from gardening supply vendors in the United States; see the Source Guide.) Any plain cooked rice will work for the stuffing. Redolent of garlic and flavorful Pecorino Romano cheese, this dish also makes a satisfying accompaniment to meaty cuts of white fish, such as halibut steaks.

2 small, thin, 7-ounce eggplants

8 ounces tomato (about 1 tomato), peeled, seeded, and diced (about 1 cup)

4 cloves garlic, chopped

6 ounces zucchini (about 1 large zucchini), chopped

$\frac{1}{2}$ cup cooked rice

2 tablespoons chopped fresh oregano

$\frac{1}{2}$ teaspoon freshly ground black pepper

$\frac{1}{4}$ teaspoon salt

2 tablespoons freshly grated Pecorino Romano cheese

2 tablespoons bread crumbs (see Pantry)

1 tablespoon chopped fresh flat-leaf parsley

Olive oil cooking spray

Preheat the oven to 400 degrees.

Cut each eggplant in half lengthwise. Leaving a $\frac{1}{4}$-inch border all around, scoop out and dice the pulp.

Preheat a medium nonstick skillet over medium-high heat. Add the tomato and garlic. Stirring constantly, cook until bubbly, about 4 minutes. Add the zucchini and the diced eggplant and cook for about 6 minutes, stirring occasionally, until soft and almost dry. Stir in the rice, oregano, black pepper, and salt.

Fill the cavity of each eggplant half with a mounded $\frac{1}{2}$ cup of the mixture. Place in a baking dish, cover, and bake for 15 minutes. Meanwhile, mix together the cheese, bread crumbs, and parsley.

Remove the baking dish from the oven. Spray the stuffed eggplants lightly with olive oil. Sprinkle each with about 4 teaspoons of the bread crumb mixture. Return to the oven and bake, uncovered, for about 15 minutes more, until browned.

Yield = 4 servings
Fat per serving = 0.99 g.
Calories per serving = 82.7

Mussels Casino

½ cup bread crumbs (see Pantry)

¼ cup chopped roasted sweet red pepper (see Pantry)

¼ cup chopped fresh flat-leaf parsley

2 teaspoons chopped fresh oregano

⅛ teaspoon finely chopped lemon zest

1 tablespoon freshly grated Parmigiano-Reggiano cheese

1 tablespoon dry white wine

2 large cloves garlic, peeled

12 green-lip mussels on the half shell (see Pantry)

Preheat the oven to 425 degrees.

In a bowl, combine the bread crumbs, roasted red pepper, parsley, oregano, lemon zest, and ½ tablespoon of the Parmesan. Stir in the wine. Press the garlic into the bowl and mix. Mound a generous 1 tablespoon of the mixture onto each mussel and top with ⅛ teaspoon cheese.

Bake for 5 minutes, then broil for 2 to 3 minutes, until well browned. Serve with lemon wedges.

Yield = 12 stuffed mussels
Fat per mussel = 0.44 g.
Calories per mussel = 23.8

MUSSELS REPLACE clams in this new twist on a classic Italian-American dish. If you use green-lip mussels, the type imported from New Zealand, preparation will be effortless. You can keep them on hand in the freezer; they're partially cooked and thus don't have to be steamed as blue mussels do, and they come already opened on the half shell. Green-lip mussels are also somewhat larger, making for a more substantial appetizer.

THIS IS OUR TAKE ON a northern Italian dish in which peppers are braised in an anchovy sauce. We roast the peppers and chill them in our sauce instead, then serve them on an arrangement of polenta crostini. Since the anchovies come packed in oil, you'll first need to rinse them and pat them dry.

Roasted Peppers with Anchovy Sauce on Polenta Crostini

1 pound red bell peppers (about 2 large peppers), halved lengthwise, cored, and seeded
1 pound yellow bell peppers (about 2 large peppers), halved lengthwise, cored, and seeded
5 anchovy fillets, rinsed, dried, and finely chopped (about 2 teaspoons)
1 teaspoon Dijon mustard

4 cloves garlic, peeled
3 tablespoons balsamic vinegar
2⅓ cups skim milk
⅔ cup buttermilk
¼ teaspoon salt
1 teaspoon sugar
1 cup coarse yellow Italian cornmeal (polenta)
Olive oil cooking spray

Preheat the broiler. Line a broiler rack with aluminum foil.

Place the peppers cut side down on the prepared rack, 2 to 3 inches from the heat source. Broil for about 5 minutes, until charred. Seal the peppers in an airtight bag for about 10 minutes, then rub their skins off, slice thin, and set aside.

In a medium glass or ceramic bowl, combine the anchovies and mustard. Press in the garlic. Mix in the vinegar. Add the peppers and mix to coat thoroughly. Cover and chill for at least 1 hour.

To make the polenta, combine the skim milk, buttermilk, salt, and sugar in a medium saucepan over medium heat (do not use a nonstick pan). Bring to a boil, then slowly stir in the cornmeal. Reduce the heat to low and cook for about 5 minutes, stirring with a wooden spoon until the mixture is thick, smooth, and separates easily from the sides of the pan. Pour into a nonstick 8-inch loaf pan, cover, and chill for 2 hours.

Preheat the broiler. Line a broiler tray with aluminum foil and coat lightly with olive oil spray.

Cut the polenta into $\frac{1}{2}$-inch slices and then cut each slice in half on the diagonal. Place on the prepared tray and broil until brown, 1 to 2 minutes per side.

Serve each person $\frac{1}{4}$ cup of the pepper mixture arranged over 4 triangles of polenta.

Yield = 8 servings
Fat per serving = 0.94 g.
Calories per serving = 118.7

Eggplant Crostini

IN THIS UNIQUE crostini, the typical slice of bread is replaced by an eggplant round, which makes for a lighter and more distinctive base. It's topped with a slice of tomato and a creamy basil and olive-flecked cheese mixture, sprinkled with bread crumbs, and browned under the broiler. We call for kalamata olives for their robust flavor, in lieu of the milder Italian varieties. Use skim milk and skim-milk ricotta cheese so that you can indulge in a bit of heavenly full-fat Parmigiano-Reggiano.

One 1½-pound purple eggplant, peeled and cut into twelve ½-inch rounds
1 tablespoon coarse salt
Olive oil cooking spray
2 kalamata olives, pitted
1 cup skim-milk ricotta cheese
½ cup packed fresh basil leaves, plus additional leaves for garnish
2 teaspoons freshly grated Parmigiano-Reggiano cheese
¼ teaspoon freshly ground black pepper
¼ teaspoon salt
2 tablespoons skim milk
Two 8-ounce tomatoes, each peeled and cut into six ¼-inch slices
1 tablespoon bread crumbs (see Pantry)

Sprinkle the eggplant rounds with the coarse salt and set them aside in a colander to drain for 1 hour.

Preheat the broiler.

Rinse the eggplant rounds, pat them dry, and place them on a broiler tray. Spray lightly with olive oil. Broil for about 5 minutes, until the eggplant is beginning to brown. Flip the rounds, spray the other side with olive oil, and broil for 3 minutes more. Remove the tray, leaving the broiler on.

In the bowl of a food processor or blender, combine the olives, ricotta, basil, Parmesan, black pepper, and salt. Turn the machine on low and add the milk through the feed tube, processing until the mixture is very smooth.

Top each broiled eggplant round with a tomato slice and spread it evenly with 1 tablespoon of the ricotta mixture. Sprinkle with ½ teaspoon bread crumbs.

Return the layered eggplant to the broiler tray and broil for 2 to 3 minutes, until browned. Remove to a serving plate and garnish with basil leaves.

Yield = 12 crostini
Fat per crostini = 0.50 g.
Calories per crostini = 39.4

Soups

(Zuppe e Minestre)

Basil, Bean, and Barley Soup ❧ Roasted Garlic and Onion Soup ❧ Seafood Soup ❧ Roasted Vegetable and Fava Bean Soup ❧ Bean and Vegetable Stew ❧ Eggplant, Tomato, and Basil Soup ❧ Butternut Squash Soup ❧ Tomato-Fennel Soup ❧ Tuscan Mussel Stew ❧ Garlic Broth

3. Soups

(Zuppe e Minestre)

Much of the appeal of Italian cooking lies in its simplicity. Italians choose the freshest ingredients and prepare them in ways that bring out their best qualities. There is no pretension, no convoluted preparation that showcases the skill of the cook even as it obliterates the essence of the food. Less is decidedly more in the Italian kitchen.

And what could be more basic than soup? In the villages and countryside of Italy, as in most cultures, soups were historically foods of the poor. They were hearty and filling, made from commodities that were easily obtained—legumes, potatoes and assorted vegetables, tomatoes, greens, and perhaps seafood, if the region was coastal. *Minestre* boasted pasta or grains as well, while bread was often added to *zuppe*.

Although soups have for years been served as a first course instead of pasta or risotto, eating habits have now gone full circle. Much like the peasants of yore, today's diners are increasingly likely to make soup the main part of their meal.

We have tried to include a range of traditional flavor combinations: barley and beans, tomato with fennel and leek, beans and mussels, zucchini and pasta, fava beans and vegetables. But we part company with tradition in our methodology. Instead of sautéing the ingredients in oil, we roast them in stock, which not only removes the fat but intensifies the flavor as well.

We also tend to puree roasted vegetables for many soups—unusual |although hardly unheard of in Italian soup-making—in the manner of a *passato.* Partly this is a matter of personal preference, partly an adaptation to the psychology of fat-free cooking: the thicker and richer the soup looks to the eye and feels on the tongue, the more satisfying it will be, with or without the use of oil or other high-fat ingredients.

One of the most popular types of soup in Italy is some combination of beans, barley, and basil, usually with some greens added to the mix. In this recipe, our green of choice is red chard, but you could easily substitute escarole, kale, or chicory, depending on preference and availability.

This is an ideal soup for the holiday season, since it's even better if you start with stock made from the Thanksgiving or Christmas turkey and throw in a little leftover meat as well. One cold and rainy December 26 on the Outer Banks, we made a huge pot with the remains of the Yule bird and mustard greens, a local favorite. It kept our friends Claudia, Deb, and Jim warm and snug for hours as we sat out a raging nor'easter.

Basil, Bean, and Barley Soup

6 ounces (about ½ bunch) red chard

6 ounces yellow onion (about 1 onion), diced (about 1 cup)

2 tablespoons plus 5 cups Chicken Stock (see Pantry)

5 ounces carrot (about 1 large carrot), peeled and cut into large dice (about ¾ cup)

12 ounces zucchini (about 2 zucchini), cut into large dice (about 2 cups)

1½ cups cooked cannellini beans (see Pantry)

⅓ cup quick-cooking pearled barley

½ cup finely chopped fresh basil

½ teaspoon freshly ground black pepper

Trim the chard, reserving the stems. Chop the leaves (about 2 cups) and the stems (about ½ cup).

Preheat a Dutch oven over high heat.

Combine the onion and 2 tablespoons of the chicken stock in the hot Dutch oven and cook, stirring, until translucent and dry, 2 to 3 minutes. Add the chard stems, carrot, zucchini, and beans. Stir in the remaining 5 cups of stock and bring to a boil over high heat. Stir in the barley. Lower the heat to medium-low, cover, and simmer for about 15 minutes, until the zucchini and barley are tender.

Remove the pot from the heat and stir in the chard leaves and the basil. Cover again and set aside for about 2 minutes, until the chard and basil have wilted. Stir in the black pepper.

Serve about 1 cup to each person.

Yield = 8 servings
Fat per serving = 0.45 g.
Calories per serving = 97.0

Roasted Garlic and Onion Soup

7 ounces garlic (about 2 heads), separated into cloves and peeled

1 pound white onions (about 2 onions), peeled and cut into 8 chunks each

1 pound leeks (2 to 3 leeks), cleaned, trimmed of dark green ends, and quartered

2 large sprigs oregano

2 cups Chicken Stock (see Pantry)

1 cup evaporated skim milk

1 teaspoon salt

½ teaspoon freshly ground black pepper

THIS CREAMY SOUP IS particularly rich and aromatic. Baking the garlic, onion, and leeks in stock achieves the same sweet caramelization that would result from browning them in oil on the stovetop. We like to place toasted slices of polenta in the soup bowls, or to float toasted polenta croutons on top of the soup.

Preheat the oven to 350 degrees.

Place the garlic, onions, and leeks in a single layer in a baking dish and top with the oregano. Pour in the stock. Cover with aluminum foil and bake for 1 hour.

Stem the oregano. In 2 batches, transfer the leaves and the remaining contents of the baking dish to a blender or food processor and puree until smooth. Transfer to a medium saucepan over medium-low heat. Add the evaporated milk, salt, and black pepper. Cook for 3 to 4 minutes to heat through, taking care not to boil.

Yield = 6 servings
Fat per serving = 0.50 g.
Calories per serving = 132.8

Seafood Soup

BARRY ADORES seafood soups of all kinds, so we've spooned our way through an abundance of bouillabaisses, cioppinos, mariscadas, and different varieties of Asian hot-pots over the years, in various parts of the world. But we keep coming back to our favorite—a *zuppa di pesce* served up at a little hole-in-the-wall Italian restaurant in Chicago that probably hasn't changed much in at least 40 years. The soup costs about three times more than anything else on the menu and is hearty enough to feed a small army.

Many Italian seafood soups we've encountered include a single fish or shellfish, although an Adriatic-style *brodetto* may be made from a dozen local varieties. Green-lip mussels are fairly large, so if you use them in this soup, cut them in half before adding them to the pot. Serve with grilled or broiled slices of Italian bread spread with roasted garlic.

4 ounces leek (about 1 thin leek), cleaned, trimmed of dark green ends, cut in half lengthwise, and sliced (about ²/₃ cup)

¼ cup dry white wine

1 whole serrano chili pepper

3 cloves garlic, minced

1 cup clam juice

2¼ pounds tomatoes (4 to 6 tomatoes), peeled, seeded, and chopped (about 3 cups), or 3 cups cut-up boxed or canned tomatoes with their juice

2 tablespoons minced fresh flat-leaf parsley

2 tablespoons chopped fresh basil

Salt and freshly ground black pepper to taste

4 ounces cooked, shelled mussels

4 ounces cleaned squid with tentacles, bodies cut into rings

4 ounces bay scallops

Preheat a Dutch oven over medium-high heat. Add the leek, wine, and chili pepper. Sauté for about 3 minutes, until the leek browns. Add the garlic and cook for 20 to 30 seconds, stirring constantly, until it begins to give off an aroma. Stir in the clam juice and tomatoes. Cover, reduce the heat to medium-low, and cook for 15 minutes.

Remove the chili pepper from the soup and stir in the parsley, basil, salt, and black pepper. Add the mussels, squid, and scallops. Cook for about 5 minutes more, until the squid and scallops turn opaque. Serve a generous 1⅓ cups to each person.

Yield = 4 servings
Fat per serving = 0.99 g.
Calories per serving = 147.8

Roasted Vegetable and Fava Bean Soup

Olive oil cooking spray

2 pounds baking potatoes (about 4 potatoes), peeled and cut into ¼-inch cubes (about 5 cups)

8 ounces carrot (about 2 carrots), peeled and diced (about 1 cup)

8 ounces yellow onion (about 2 small onions), diced (about 1⅓ cups)

12 ounces celery (about 4 stalks), trimmed and diced (about 1 cup)

12 ounces plum tomatoes (about 4 tomatoes), peeled and seeded (about 1⅓ cups)

4 cups water

½ teaspoon salt plus additional to taste

2 pounds fava beans, shelled

2 ounces arugula, stemmed and chopped (about 1 cup, packed)

4 cups Vegetable Stock (see page 20)

Freshly ground black pepper to taste

2 tablespoons chopped fresh flat-leaf parsley

Preheat the oven to 400 degrees. Spray a baking sheet lightly with the olive oil.

Arrange the potatoes, carrots, onions, celery, and tomatoes in a single layer on the prepared sheet. Roast for 10 minutes, spray the vegetables with olive oil, toss, and bake until well browned, about 20 minutes more.

In a medium saucepan, bring the water to a boil over high heat. Add ½ teaspoon salt and the fava beans. Cook for 30 seconds, drain, and rinse under cold water. Peel the beans.

In a large saucepan, combine the roasted vegetables, fava beans, arugula, and stock. Bring to a boil, reduce the heat to low, cover, and simmer for about 15 minutes to allow the flavors to blend. Add salt and black pepper.

Ladle 1 cup into each of 6 serving bowls. Garnish each with 1 teaspoon of the chopped parsley.

Yield = 6 servings
Fat per serving = 0.68 g.
Calories per serving = 167.2

WE LIKE TO PUT A slice of toasted Italian bread in each bowl before ladling in this soup, and place a wedge of Parmigiano-Reggiano on the dining table to be grated into individual servings. The roasted potatoes hold their shape and texture well in this recipe, whereas in many long-cooking soups much of the potato disintegrates and serves more as a thickener than as a distinct element. Taste the soup before you add pepper, since the arugula already lends a peppery bite.

Bean and Vegetable Stew

We LIKE BEAN AND Vegetable Stew paired with so many pastas that it's easy to forget just how satisfying it is by itself. It makes a particularly good home for our Ricotta and Basil Tortellini (page 113). Another tasty variation is to stir in up to 1½ cups of a cooked, small, shaped pasta, such as farfalle, conchiglielle shells, or orecchiette, along with the beans; you could also add orzo.

Olive oil cooking spray

4 ounces eggplant (about 1 baby eggplant), cut into ¼-inch cubes (about ¾ cup)

4 ounces zucchini (about 1 small zucchini), cut into matchsticks (about ¾ cup)

2 ounces leek (about 1 baby leek, white and light green parts only), cleaned and cut into rings (about ¼ cup)

3 ounces carrot (about 1 carrot), peeled and cut into matchsticks (about ½ cup)

Three 1-ounce cremini mushrooms, cleaned, trimmed, and cut into eighths

8 ounces plum tomatoes (about 2 tomatoes), peeled, seeded, and cut into ¼-inch cubes (about ¾ cup)

2 cups Vegetable Stock (see page 20)

1½ cups cooked cannellini beans (see Pantry)

2 tablespoons chopped fresh flat-leaf parsley

Preheat the oven to 400 degrees. Spray a baking sheet lightly with olive oil.

Put the eggplant on the prepared baking sheet and spray once again with the oil. Bake for about 10 minutes, until browned.

In a large saucepan, combine the browned eggplant, zucchini, leek, carrot, mushrooms, plum tomatoes, and Vegetable Stock. Bring to a boil over high heat, then lower the heat and simmer for about 10 minutes, until the carrot is soft. Stir in the beans and parsley and cook for about 5 minutes more to heat through.

In each of 4 bowls, ladle a generous 1 cup of stew.

Yield = 4 servings
Fat per serving = 0.65 g.
Calories per serving = 123.4

Eggplant, Tomato, and Basil Soup

1½ pounds purple eggplant (about 1 eggplant), cut in half lengthwise

2 pounds tomatoes (about 4 tomatoes), halved, cored, and seeded

8 cloves garlic, peeled and crushed

3½ cups Vegetable Stock (see page 20)

1 cup packed fresh basil leaves

3 tablespoons sun-dried tomato paste

1 tablespoon balsamic vinegar

¼ teaspoon freshly ground black pepper

Salt to taste

1 small fresh red chili pepper, cored, seeded, and deveined (optional)

Preheat the oven to 350 degrees.

Place the eggplant, tomatoes, and garlic in a baking dish in a single layer and pour the stock over the vegetables. Cover and bake for 1 hour.

Remove from the oven and allow to cool. Peel the eggplant and tomatoes and put them, in batches, in a blender or food processor along with the remaining contents of the baking dish. Add the basil, tomato paste, vinegar, black pepper, salt, and chili pepper (if desired) and puree.

Transfer to a large saucepan and heat over medium-high heat for 3 to 4 minutes, until steaming.

Serve about 1 cup to each person.

Yield = 8 servings
Fat per serving = 0.35 g.
Calories per serving = 59.7

IN THIS RECIPE, THE traditional Italian combination of eggplant and tomatoes receives a contemporary flavor boost from sun-dried tomato paste, balsamic vinegar, and a chili pepper. The skins will slip right off the eggplant and tomatoes after they come out of the oven. The soup is fairly dense; if you prefer a slightly thinner version, stir in up to 1 cup of additional Vegetable Stock after pureeing and warm for a minute or two more.

Butternut Squash Soup

TENDER AMERICAN butternut squash tastes much like the orange flesh of the Chioggia squash found in Italy. It's the star of this creamless soup, which derives its creamy texture from a puree of roasted squash, onion, garlic, and, for sweetness, apple. A dollop of yogurt added just before serving makes an attractive garnish against the pretty yellow-orange of the squash and thickens the soup even more as it dissolves. We add coriander, not a particularly Italian accent, just because it goes so well with the squash.

2½ pounds butternut squash (about 2 small squash), cut in half lengthwise and seeded
1 pound yellow onions (about 2 onions), peeled and quartered
1 pound Granny Smith apples (about 2 apples), halved and cored
2 ounces garlic (about 8 large cloves), peeled and crushed

3½ cups Vegetable Stock (see page 20)
½ teaspoon ground coriander
¼ teaspoon cayenne pepper
¼ teaspoon salt
½ cup plain nonfat yogurt
2 teaspoons chopped fresh oregano

Preheat the oven to 350 degrees.

Arrange the squash, onions, apples, and garlic in a single layer in a baking dish. Add the stock. Cover and bake for 1 hour.

Remove from the oven and allow to cool. Peel the apples and squash. Combine them in a blender or food processor with the remaining contents of the baking dish and puree until very smooth. Transfer to a large saucepan and add the coriander, cayenne, and salt. Warm over medium heat for 2 to 3 minutes, until steaming.

Serve 1 cup to each person. Garnish each portion with 1 tablespoon yogurt and ¼ teaspoon chopped oregano.

Yield = 8 servings
Fat per serving = 0.45 g.
Calories per serving = 121.6

Tomato-Fennel Soup

1 pound plum tomatoes (4 to 5 tomatoes), quartered

1 pound fennel (about 1 bulb), trimmed and quartered, feathery ends reserved

2 ounces leek (about 1 baby leek), cleaned, trimmed, and quartered lengthwise

2½ cups Vegetable Stock (see page 20)

1 tablespoon tomato paste

½ teaspoon salt

¼ teaspoon freshly ground black pepper

THIS ROBUST SOUP IS pureed to a silky consistency. It's almost effortless to make, using our favorite method for preparing vegetable soups— oven-baking the ingredients in the stock. This method dispenses with the laborious first step of chopping the vegetables, intensifies their flavor, and basically lets the oven do the cooking. The soup only needs to be finished and warmed through on the stovetop.

Preheat the oven to 350 degrees.

Place the tomatoes, fennel, and leek in a baking dish in a single layer. Add the stock. Cover and bake for 1 hour.

Remove the tomatoes and peel their skins. Combine the peeled tomatoes in a blender with the remaining contents of the baking dish. Puree until smooth and transfer to a medium saucepan over medium-low heat. Stir in the tomato paste and cook for 4 to 5 minutes, until steaming. Stir in the salt and pepper.

Serve a generous cup to each person and garnish each portion with about ½ teaspoon of the reserved fennel greens.

Yield = 4 servings
Fat per serving = 0.45 g.
Calories per serving = 56.4

Tuscan Mussel Stew

THIS IS OUR ATTEMPT to simplify a classic dish, as well as to strip it of the usual dose of oil. (We've even come across Americanized versions that include oil *and* butter.) In just about every other recipe we've seen, each of several components for the soup cooks in a separate pot, but we cook them all together. We also like to leave the mussels in their shells rather than shelling them at some point before serving. This dish is even easier if you start with debearded mussels, which are usually packaged in mesh bags at the supermarket fish counter.

And of course this stew is brimming with cannellinis. The Tuscans are so fond of legumes that people in other regions of Italy refer to them as "the bean eaters."

6 cloves garlic, chopped
3/4 cup dry white wine
1 pound tomatoes (about 2 tomatoes), peeled, seeded, and diced (about 1 1/2 cups), or 1 1/2 cups cut-up boxed or canned tomatoes with their juice
1 teaspoon Dried Seasoning Blend (see page 22)

1 1/2 cups cooked cannellini beans (see Pantry)
1 cup Vegetable Stock (see page 20)
1/8 teaspoon crushed red pepper flakes
2 tablespoons chopped fresh flat-leaf parsley
2 pounds debearded blue mussels

Preheat a nonstick Dutch oven over high heat. Add the garlic and 1/4 cup of the wine. Stirring constantly, cook until the garlic becomes aromatic, 30 to 45 seconds. Add the tomatoes, seasoning blend, beans, Vegetable Stock, crushed pepper, parsley, mussels, and the remaining 1/2 cup wine. Cover and cook for about 8 minutes, periodically shaking the pan, until the mussels have opened.

Serve about 3/4 cup of soup to each person, dividing the mussels equally (the number can vary greatly depending on size).

Yield = 6 servings
Fat per serving = 0.91 g.
Calories per serving = 125.4

Garlic Broth

9 ounces zucchini (1 to 2 zucchini)

½ teaspoon coarse salt

Olive oil cooking spray

4 cups Vegetable Stock (see page 20)

12 cloves garlic, peeled

½ cup chopped arugula

Trim and cut the zucchini in half lengthwise, then cut it crosswise into ¼ inch-thick slices, creating half-moons. Place the zucchini in a colander, sprinkle with the salt, and let sit for 30 minutes. Rinse and squeeze dry with paper towels.

Preheat the oven to 400 degrees. Spray a baking sheet twice with olive oil.

Arrange the zucchini in a single layer on the prepared baking sheet. Bake for 10 minutes. Turn the slices and bake for about 5 minutes more, until browned and crisp. Remove from the oven and allow to cool on the sheet.

Combine the stock and garlic in a medium saucepan over medium heat. Cook until the garlic becomes aromatic, about 10 minutes. Remove and discard the garlic.

Into each of 4 bowls, ladle 1 cup of broth and top with 2 tablespoons of the arugula and 1½ tablespoons of the zucchini.

Yield = 4 servings
Fat per serving = 0.23 g.
Calories per serving = 43.2

A LIGHT YET intensely flavorful broth, or *brodo*, this is equally good by itself and as a foil for various types of delicate additions. It is a perfect soup in which to float small stuffed pasta, such as our Shrimp and Zucchini Agnolotti (page 112) or Roasted Tomato Ravioli (page 116). It also makes a very good base for a savory flan; try it with our Artichoke Flan (page 32) in place of the broth included in that recipe. Garlic Broth takes on a subtle personality change when you substitute thinly sliced or chopped escarole or spinach for the arugula.

Bread

(Pane)

Traditional Italian Sponge ～ Rustic Italian Bread ～
Rosemary Bread with Sea Salt Topping ～ Sardinian Flat
Bread ～ Grissini ～ Yeast Starter ～ Anise Bread ～
Soft Breadsticks ～ Almond-Glazed Panettone ～
Milanese Panettone

4. Bread

(Pane)

The days when the aroma of baking bread wafted from communal ovens in the center of Italian villages may be past, but bread still plays a fundamental role in daily life. Bread is so central to dining that Italians use the term *companatico* to refer to foods that accompany the bread.

Omnipresent, a staple throughout the Italian meal rather than a prelude in the American fashion, bread is a constant in a changing world. Health-conscious Italians might skip the antipasti or *dolci* in everyday home cooking, but never the *pane*.

We offer several variations on very good, basic Italian baker's loaves, including those with rosemary and anise flavorings and a soft breadstick. For people with a sweet tooth, there are two renditions of panettone. Crispy breadsticks, called *grissini,* and a papery thin flat-bread round out the chapter.

In all recipes, the dictates of a fat-free kitchen prohibit the use of oil other than when needed to lightly coat a bowl or pan, and additions of cheese, seeds, and other fatty ingredients are kept to a minimum. For sweet yeast-raised breads, full-fat dairy products are replaced with skim milk, buttermilk, egg whites, and egg substitute made from egg whites.

With the exception of panettone, which mixes better in a stationary electric mixer, we have tailored our breads to be made in the food processor. These days, working families who choose to cook at home—and who make the extra effort to cook fat-free—deserve baking recipes that are as accessible and unthreatening as they can be. The food-processing method of mixing doughs is the most foolproof, and the machine does the kneading for you as well. We've tried to make these recipes simple and reliable. Follow them carefully, and don't be nervous about trying yeast breads.

Most yeast breads will keep for 2 or 3 days, *grissini* and flat bread even longer, if they are loosely wrapped in aluminum foil. Double-wrapped in plastic, panettone will keep for up to 2 weeks in the refrigerator; bring it back to room temperature before serving.

Traditional Italian Sponge

Taking the extra first step of fermenting a sponge starter for a few hours yields an infinitely more flavorful bread, one with a decided tang and a distinctive personality. Use this sponge to make Rustic Italian Bread (page 63) and Rosemary Bread (page 64).

The starter is similar to that used by our friend and colleague Jill Van Cleave in the Italian baker's loaf she created for *The Neighborhood Bakeshop*. She tells the story of visiting her favorite Italian baker, Ciro Pasciuto, who migrated from Gaeta, near Naples, to Seattle. When Jill left, Ciro handed her a bag filled with his bread, which he advised her not to eat until she had been home for a few hours, since "it will have more character after it gets used to the new surroundings."

½ teaspoon active dry yeast
¼ cup lukewarm water (105 to 115 degrees on an instant-read thermometer)

1 cup room-temperature water
2 cups bread flour

Dissolve the yeast in the lukewarm water in a large ceramic or glass mixing bowl. Let it stand until uniformly creamy, about 10 minutes. Stir in the room-temperature water. Stir in the flour 1 cup at a time, mixing well after each addition, to form a dough. Cover tightly with plastic wrap and set aside at room temperature for at least 6 to 7 hours (or for up to 12 hours), until the sponge is bubbly and has tripled in size and then receded slightly in the center.

The sponge can be covered with plastic wrap and stored in the refrigerator for up to 24 hours. Bring back to room temperature before using.

Yield = Enough dough for two 13-inch loaves

Rustic Italian Bread

1 prepared recipe Traditional Italian
   Sponge (page 62)
$\frac{1}{4}$ cup room-temperature water
1 teaspoon sugar

2 teaspoons salt
2 cups bread flour
3 tablespoons cornmeal

Scrape the sponge into the bowl of a food processor. Add the water, sugar, salt, and 1 cup of the flour. Pulse 10 times. Add the remaining 1 cup flour. Process for about 15 seconds, until a dough ball just begins to form. Scrape the dough onto a lightly floured work surface and knead it together into a ball. Transfer the ball to a large, ungreased ceramic or glass bowl and cover the bowl tightly with plastic wrap. Set aside for about 1½ hours, until the dough has doubled in size and does not spring back to the touch.

Line a baking sheet with parchment paper and sprinkle it with the cornmeal.

Divide the dough in half and place it on a lightly floured work surface. Form each half into a 13-inch loaf about 1½ inches high. Place the loaves on the prepared sheet and cover loosely with a clean, dry dish towel. Set aside to rise again until doubled in size, about 45 minutes.

Preheat the oven to 450 degrees. Preheat a baking stone if desired.

Transfer the loaves from the parchment-lined sheet to the baking stone or set the baking sheet in the oven. Spritz the loaves lightly with water. Bake for 5 minutes, open the oven door, and spritz the loaves lightly again. Bake for 5 minutes more and repeat the process. Reduce the oven temperature to 400 degrees and bake for about 20 minutes more, until the loaves are light golden and sound hollow when tapped on the bottom.

Yield = Two 13-inch loaves, or about fifty-two ½-inch slices
Fat per slice = 0.09 g.
Calories per slice = 32.1

THIS RECIPE YIELDS crusty, rough-hewn loaves with centers that are somewhat denser than usual, because of our use of high-gluten bread flour. Spritzing adds the moisture that produces a crustier bread. You can also achieve this by positioning an ovenproof dish in the bottom of the oven when you preheat it, placing 2 or 3 ice cubes in the dish when the bread goes into the oven, and then placing 2 or 3 more ice cubes in it after 5 minutes of baking. Using a baking stone will yield bread a bit crustier still—more like that produced in a professional baker's brick oven.

Rosemary Bread with Sea Salt Topping

2 cups unbleached all-purpose flour
1 teaspoon sugar
1 tablespoon chopped fresh rosemary
2 teaspoons salt

1 prepared recipe Traditional Italian Sponge (page 62)
1/4 cup room-temperature water
1 tablespoon sea salt crystals

Combine the flour, sugar, rosemary, and salt in the bowl of a food processor. Process for about 10 seconds to aerate and combine. Scrape in the sponge. Turn the machine on and drizzle the water through the feed tube to form a dough ball. Continue to process until the ball has made 30 revolutions. (It will turn slowly at the outset.) Transfer the dough to a large, ungreased ceramic or glass bowl and cover the bowl tightly with plastic wrap. Set aside for 1 1/2 to 1 3/4 hours, until the dough has doubled in size and does not spring back to the touch.

Transfer the dough to a lightly floured work surface. Cut it in half and form each half into a 13-inch loaf, about 1 1/2 inches high. Place the loaves in the wells of a nonstick French bread pan. Cover loosely with a clean, dry dish towel and set aside to double in size again, about 45 minutes.

Preheat the oven to 400 degrees.

Make 3 diagonal slashes in the top of each loaf with a razor blade or a sharp knife. Spritz the loaves lightly with some of the water and sprinkle them with the salt crystals. Put 3 ice cubes directly on the bottom of the oven. Bake the loaves for 5 minutes, spritz the loaves again, and add 2 more ice cubes. Bake for about 30 minutes more, until the loaves are dark golden and sound hollow when tapped on the bottom.

Yield = Two 13-inch loaves, or about fifty-two 1/2-inch slices
Fat per slice = 0.08 g.
Calories per slice = 30.3

Sardinian Flat Bread

1½ cups semolina flour
1 cup unbleached all-purpose flour
¼ teaspoon sugar

½ tablespoon salt
1 cup water

Combine the flours, sugar, and salt in a food processor and process for about 15 seconds to mix. With the machine running, slowly add the water through the feed tube to form a dough ball. Continue to process for an additional minute or two. Remove to a very lightly floured work surface and knead 5 to 10 times, until smooth and elastic. Wrap in plastic wrap and set aside for 1 hour.

Preheat the oven to 450 degrees.

Unwrap the dough and cut it into 6 equal pieces. Roll each out into a paper-thin 12-by-10-inch rectangular sheet. Lay the rectangles flat on ungreased baking sheets. Bake for 3 minutes, until slightly firmed, then flip the dough and bake for about 3 minutes more to brown lightly. Remove to wire racks to cool. Repeat the process until all the dough is baked. Break each sheet into 4 smaller pieces.

Yield = 24 pieces
Fat per piece = 0.20 g.
Calories per piece = 54.1

CALLED *CARTA DA musica* because it is as thin and brittle as the paper on which music was traditionally printed, this rustic-looking bread is rather like an ethereal lavasch. The sheets make a good base for Tuna Pâté (page 37), Caponata (page 34), Sardine Paste (page 39), and other savory toppings.

Grissini

1 teaspoon active dry yeast

¼ cup lukewarm water (105 to 115 degrees on an instant-read thermometer)

1 teaspoon salt

2 teaspoons freshly grated Parmigiano-Reggiano cheese

1¾ cups unbleached all-purpose flour

½ cup room-temperature water

Olive oil cooking spray

2 tablespoons cornmeal

These traditional crispy breadsticks contain just a hint of Parmesan cheese. As you guide the strands of dough out of the pasta machine and transfer them to the baking sheet, they seem to take on a life of their own, ending up stretched thin in places, bunched up a bit and bent askew in others. Pay no heed, as this will only lend charm to the finished product. You can also form the *grissini* by hand by cutting the 12-by-5-inch rectangle of dough into 48 strips, each ¼ inch by 5 inches, and then rolling each strip into a 9-inch rope. In this case, bake for about 20 minutes.

Sometimes we like to replace the cornmeal sprinkled on the baking sheet with poppy seeds or sesame seeds and roll the strips gently in the seeds to coat them. Serve the breadsticks standing straight up in glasses, spewing from baskets, or simply piled on a corner of the table.

Combine the yeast and the lukewarm water in a small bowl. Stir and let sit for 8 to 10 minutes, until bubbly.

In the bowl of a food processor, combine the salt, Parmesan cheese, and 1½ cups of the flour. Pulse a few times to mix. Scrape in the yeast mixture. Turn the machine on and slowly add the room-temperature water until a dough ball forms. (You may not need to use the full ½ cup.) Continue to process for about 45 seconds more. Transfer the dough to a large glass or ceramic bowl lightly coated with olive oil spray, cover the bowl tightly with plastic wrap, and allow the dough to double in size, about 1 to 1¼ hours.

Preheat the oven to 400 degrees. Sprinkle a large baking sheet with the cornmeal.

Use the remaining ¼ cup flour to coat a work surface. Remove the dough to the floured surface and work it into a 12-by-5-inch rectangle. Cut the rectangle into 3 pieces, each 4 inches by 5 inches, and put each piece through the fettuccine cutters on a pasta machine. Arrange the strands on the prepared baking sheet.

Bake for 15 minutes. Remove those breadsticks that have turned golden and return the rest to the oven for another 2 to 3 minutes to color.

Yield = About 48 breadsticks
Fat per breadstick = 0.06 g.
Calories per breadstick = 15.9

Yeast Starter

¾ cup room-temperature water

¾ teaspoon active dry yeast

¼ teaspoon sugar

1 cup unbleached all-purpose flour

In a large ceramic or glass bowl, combine ¼ cup of the water, the yeast, and the sugar. Let stand for 5 to 10 minutes, until creamy.

Add the remaining ½ cup water and the flour. Stir with a wooden spoon to make a soft, smooth, pasty dough. Cover with plastic wrap and set aside for 8 to 12 hours, until about tripled in size and bubbly.

Punch the dough to deflate it before using.

Yield = Enough dough for two 11-inch loaves or twenty-four 9-inch breadsticks

THE SUGAR IN THIS yeast mixture produces a much more active (more vigorously bubbling) starter than our Traditional Italian Sponge (page 62). Combined with all-purpose rather than bread flour, it results in a lighter bread dotted with more air holes. The starter can be covered with plastic wrap and stored in the refrigerator for up to 24 hours; bring it back to room temperature before using.

Anise Bread

ANISE IS A FAVORITE flavoring throughout Italy. Although many anise breads we've sampled have been on the sweet side, this one is rather more savory in character. It's very good spread with Roasted Garlic (page 14).

The best place to set doughs aside to rise is in a warm (75 to 85 degrees), draft-free spot. We usually place our doughs on top of the refrigerator or on top of the water heater in a utility closet. Remember that yeast loves humidity; keep the air conditioning and fans to a minimum on bread-baking days.

3¼ cups unbleached all-purpose flour

2 teaspoons sugar

1 teaspoon salt

1 tablespoon anise seed

¼ cup currants

1 prepared recipe Yeast Starter (page 67)

1 cup room-temperature water

2 tablespoons semolina flour

Combine the flour, sugar, salt, anise seed, and currants in the bowl of a food processor. Pulse 7 or 8 times to combine. Scrape in the starter. Turn the machine on and drizzle the water through the feed tube until a dough ball forms. (You may not need to use the full 1 cup water.) Continue to process until the ball has made 30 revolutions. Transfer the dough to a large, ungreased ceramic or glass bowl and cover the bowl tightly with plastic wrap. Set aside for 2 to 2¼ hours, until the dough has doubled in size and does not spring back to the touch.

Line a baking sheet with parchment paper and dust with the semolina.

Transfer the dough to a lightly floured work surface and cut it in half. Flatten and work each half into an 11-by-6-inch rectangle, then roll up each rectangle into an 11-inch log. Place the loaves on the prepared baking sheet seam side down. Cover loosely with a clean, dry dish towel and set aside to double in size again, about 1¼ hours.

Preheat the oven to 400 degrees.

Make 3 diagonal slashes in the top of each loaf with a razor blade or a sharp knife. Bake for about 35 minutes, until the loaves are dark golden and sound hollow when tapped on the bottom.

Yield = Two 11-inch loaves, or about forty-four ½-inch slices
Fat per slice = 0.11 g.
Calories per slice = 42.2

Soft Breadsticks

1 prepared recipe Yeast Starter (page 67)

2½ cups unbleached all-purpose flour

½ tablespoon salt

2 teaspoons dried oregano

1 cup plus 2 tablespoons room-temperature water

Olive oil cooking spray

2 tablespoons sesame seeds

THESE ARE MORE LIKE elongated rolls than typically crisp breadsticks. For variety, you could easily replace the sesame seeds with an equal amount of sea salt crystals, poppy seeds, fennel seeds, caraway seeds, or dehydrated onion flakes, or with a light sprinkling of crushed or coarsely ground black pepper.

Scrape the starter into the bowl of a food processor. Add the flour, salt, and oregano. Turn the machine on and slowly pour the water through the feed tube to form a dough ball. Remove the dough to a lightly floured work surface and knead until smooth and elastic, about 2 minutes.

Spray a large ceramic or glass bowl lightly with the olive oil and spread the oil over the surface to coat. Place the dough in the bowl and cover the bowl tightly with plastic wrap. Set it aside for about 1½ hours, until the dough has doubled in size and does not spring back to the touch.

Line a baking sheet with parchment paper.

On a lightly floured work surface, flatten the dough and form it into a 12-by-6-inch rectangle. Quarter the rectangle and cut each quarter crosswise into 6 strips, each 1 inch by 3 inches. Using the palms of your hands, roll and stretch each strip into a 9-inch rope. Place the ropes of dough on the prepared sheet and cover them loosely with a clean, dry dish towel. Set aside to rise again until doubled in size, about 30 minutes.

Preheat the oven to 425 degrees.

Spritz the breadsticks lightly with water and sprinkle ¼ teaspoon of the sesame seeds over each. Bake for 15 to 18 minutes, until the breadsticks are light golden and sound hollow when tapped on the bottom.

Yield = Twenty-four 9-inch breadsticks
Fat per breadstick = 0.52 g.
Calories per breadstick = 61.3

Almond-Glazed Panettone

BOASTING A CRUNCHY glaze and lacking the typical candied fruit, this is our low-fat version of a panettone featured by baker extraordinaire Nick Malgieri in his *Great Italian Desserts*. The original hails from Aosta, in the far northwestern corner of Italy, and reflects the influence of nearby France. Our version employs such fat-reducing substitutions as buttermilk for butter and egg-white-based egg substitute for whole eggs. To re-create the traditional topping of ground almonds, we grind a nutty cereal to yield a similar texture and flavor the topping with almond extract.

SPONGE STARTER:
1/2 cup unbleached all-purpose flour
1 packet (1/4 ounce) active dry yeast
1/3 cup lukewarm water (105 to 115 degrees on an instant-read thermometer)

DOUGH:
6 tablespoons buttermilk
1/2 teaspoon salt
1/4 cup sugar
1 tablespoon vanilla extract
3/4 cup nonfat liquid egg substitute

2 cups unbleached all-purpose flour
3/4 cup golden raisins

Olive oil cooking spray

GLAZE:
1/3 cup Grape-Nuts Flakes cereal
1/4 cup sugar
1 teaspoon cornstarch
1/2 teaspoon almond extract
1 large egg white

2 tablespoons confectioners' sugar

To make the sponge starter, put the flour into a large ceramic or glass bowl. In a small bowl, whisk the yeast into the lukewarm water. Stir the combination into the flour with a wooden spoon, cover, and set aside for about 45 minutes, until about doubled in size.

To make the dough, combine the buttermilk and salt in the bowl of a stationary electric mixer fitted with the flat paddle attachment. Mix to incorporate at low speed. Beat in the sugar and vanilla. Alternately mix in the egg substitute and the flour in increments, ending with flour. Beat in the sponge starter and continue to mix until smoothly blended. Mix in the raisins. Scrape into a large ceramic or glass bowl lightly coated with olive oil spray. Cover the bowl tightly with plastic wrap and set it aside for about 1 1/2 hours, until the dough has doubled in size.

Scrape the dough into a 9-inch springform pan that has been sprayed lightly with olive oil. With a spatula, spread the dough over the bottom. Cover the pan loosely with a clean kitchen towel and let the dough rise to the top, about 2 hours.

Meanwhile, make the glaze. Combine the Grape-Nuts Flakes and sugar in the bowl of a food processor. Pulse to grind fine, remove to a bowl, and stir in the cornstarch, almond extract, and egg white.

Preheat the oven to 375 degrees.

Gently spread the glaze over the top of the panettone and dust it with the confectioners' sugar. Bake for about 50 minutes, until a tester inserted in the center comes out clean. Remove from the oven, release the sides of the pan, and slide the bread onto a wire rack to cool.

Wrap the loaves in aluminum foil to store at room temperature for up to 3 days.

Yield = 20 servings
Fat per serving = 0.20 g.
Calories per serving = 101.5

Milanese Panettone

We'll never forget our first visit to Milan; it was at Christmastime many years ago. The city was alive with festive decorations and displays of alluring holiday sweets, including the tall, candied-citrus- and raisin-studded egg breads called panettone, which seemed to be everywhere. Some were even fancifully done up to resemble mountaintop scenes.

Although you can bake this in a soufflé mold, a panettone mold—or, perhaps a bit more practical, a washed and dried 23-ounce coffee can—will yield a panettone of more traditional proportions. For variety, replace the candied citron and orange peel with 1 cup of mixed candied fruit and peel.

SPONGE STARTER:

1 cup unbleached all-purpose flour

2/3 cup skim milk

1 tablespoon active dry yeast

DOUGH:

1 tablespoon active dry yeast

1/3 cup lukewarm water (105 to 115 degrees on an instant-read thermometer)

3/4 cup buttermilk

1/2 cup sugar

4 cups unbleached all-purpose flour

1 cup nonfat liquid egg substitute

1 teaspoon salt

2 teaspoons grated lemon zest

1 tablespoon vanilla extract

1/4 teaspoon anise extract

1/2 cup diced candied citron

1/2 cup diced candied orange peel

1 cup golden raisins

Olive oil cooking spray

1 large egg white beaten with 1 teaspoon water

For the sponge starter, put the flour into a large ceramic or glass bowl. In a small saucepan, warm the skim milk over low heat until it is lukewarm (105 to 115 degrees). Remove from the heat and whisk in the yeast. Pour over the flour and stir to create a thick, pasty dough. Cover the bowl with plastic wrap and let the starter rise for about 45 minutes, until doubled in size.

To make the dough, combine the yeast and lukewarm water in a small bowl. Set aside for about 5 minutes, until bubbly.

Combine the buttermilk and sugar in the bowl of a stationary electric mixer fitted with the flat paddle attachment. Beat at low speed until smoothly blended. Beat in 1/2 cup of the flour and the liquid egg substitute, then the salt, lemon zest, vanilla, and anise extract. Beat in another 1/2 cup flour. With the machine still running, scrape in the yeast mixture. Add the sponge starter and mix to blend well. Add 2 1/2 cups more flour, a bit at a time. Mix in the candied fruit and the raisins.

Replace the flat paddle with the dough hook and turn the machine back on to low speed. Mix for 8 minutes, gradually adding the remaining 1/2 cup flour to form a smooth, elastic dough that is still sticky to the touch. Lightly coat a large ceramic or glass bowl and a sheet of plastic wrap with olive oil spray. Place the dough in the bowl. Cover the bowl tightly with the plastic wrap (oiled side down) and set it aside for about $1\frac{1}{2}$ hours, until the dough has doubled in size.

Transfer the dough to a lightly floured work surface and cut it in half. Work each half into a smooth round. Put each round in the bottom of a 6-inch panettone mold, a rinsed and dried 23-ounce coffee can, or a $1\frac{1}{2}$-quart soufflé mold coated lightly with olive oil spray. Spray a sheet of plastic wrap lightly and cover the dough loosely. Let it rise slightly above the tops of the molds, $1\frac{1}{2}$ to 2 hours.

Preheat the oven to 375 degrees.

Using scissors that have been dipped in flour, snip an X into the top of each panettone. Paint the tops with the egg-white-and-water mixture. Bake for about 40 minutes, until the tops are well browned and a tester inserted into the center comes out clean.

Remove the panettone to a wire rack and cool for 15 to 20 minutes before unmolding, then allow the bread to cool completely on the rack.

Yield = 2 loaves, or about 20 servings
Fat per serving = 0.34 g.
Calories per serving = 93.2

Risotto

(Risotto)

Parmesan Risotto ⁓ Risotto Cakes ⁓ Barley Risotto ⁓ Lemon Risotto ⁓ Roasted Yellow Pepper Risotto ⁓ Spinach Risotto ⁓ Artichoke Risotto ⁓ Mushroom Risotto ⁓ Quail-Leek Risotto ⁓ Risotto al Barolo

5. Risotto

(Risotto)

Long a popular alternative to pasta or soup for the Italian first course, especially in the north, where rice is cultivated abundantly, risotto has taken on almost mythic dimensions over the years. Far more than mere rice, risotto borders on being a ritual.

It is also, contrary to popular belief, a dish that can easily be made fat-free. Instead of starting by browning the *soffritto* and then the rice in oil or butter, you can sauté the onion-and-garlic mixture and then the rice in wine, water, or the vegetables' own juices.

The other popular misconception about risotto is the extent to which it is a labor-intensive dish to prepare. It does take some attention, but *not* nonstop stirring. A little vigorous stirring with each addition of liquid will do just fine.

The choice of rice is critical to achieving the ideal creamy texture while maintaining some firmness in the individual grains. You can, of course, use Arborio rice, which is readily available, but our first choice would be Vialone Nano rice, which produces the creamiest, most heavenly risottos we've ever had. Our second choice is either Carnaroli or Cal Riso, a new cross between Italian and Californian rice varieties that closely resembles the Carnaroli strain.

Almost anyone who makes risotto with any frequency has a favorite risotto pot; ours is a 2-quart sauté pan. Select a heavy, wide-mouthed sauté pan or Dutch oven—a shape that will evenly distribute heat, hasten the absorption of liquid, and maximize the amount of starch the rice gives off and hence the creaminess. We also like to prepare risotto in a pressure cooker, which speeds up the process, virtually eliminates stirring, and produces consistently good results.

Our risotto portions are those of an Italian first course. A recipe that serves 6 as a first course or, in a more typically American style, as a side dish, would make a main course for 4.

Parmesan Risotto

THIS IS ONE OF THE simplest and most basic risottos. The quality of the cheese is critical; this is not the time to substitute a lesser alternative for Parmigiano-Reggiano. We like the dish with Veal Spiedini (page 154), but it really complements a wide range of main courses, as long as they don't contain any Parmesan themselves. For the ultimate luxury, top Parmesan Risotto with shaved or sliced truffles.

6 cups Beef Stock (see page 21), or 4 cups commercial beef broth plus 2 cups water

4 ounces leek (about 1 thin leek), trimmed, cleaned, quartered lengthwise, and thinly sliced (about ½ cup)

2 tablespoons water

2 cups Vialone Nano, Carnaroli, or Arborio rice

Salt and freshly ground black pepper to taste

3 tablespoons freshly grated Parmigiano-Reggiano cheese

In a medium saucepan, bring the stock to a boil. Adjust the heat to maintain a simmer.

Meanwhile, preheat a large, heavy-bottomed pan over medium heat. Add the leek and water. Sauté for about 3 minutes, until the leek is soft and most of the water has evaporated. Add the rice and continue to cook and stir for about 3 minutes more, until the rice is very lightly toasted.

Vigorously stir in 1 cup of the hot stock. Once the liquid has been absorbed and small craters dot the creamy surface, add 1 cup more. Stir and bring back to a simmer. When this addition has been absorbed, add the rest of the stock ½ cup at a time, stirring after each addition. Continue to stir until the risotto is creamy and tender. This should take 25 to 30 minutes from the first addition of stock.

Stir in the salt, black pepper, and Parmesan and serve 1 cup to each person.

Yield = 6 servings
Fat per serving = 0.73 g.
Calories per serving = 261.2

Risotto Cakes

2 cups leftover risotto, chilled   Olive oil cooking spray

With moistened hands, form the risotto into four 3½-inch patties about ½ inch thick. (Use ½ cup risotto for each patty.) Spray the top of each patty lightly with olive oil.

Preheat a large nonstick skillet or griddle over high heat. Place the patties sprayed side down on the hot skillet or griddle. Cook until well browned on the bottom, 6 to 7 minutes. Spray the tops of the patties, turn them over, and cook until well browned on the other side, about 5 minutes.

Yield = 4 servings
Fat per serving = 0.46 g.
Calories per serving = 131.4

WE'VE BECOME SO fond of Risotto Cakes that we purposely plan to have leftover risotto. You can use almost any risotto, although we think the simple Parmesan Risotto probably produces the best result. To highlight the flavor, grate a little fresh Parmesan cheese over the top of each cake after flipping it to cook on the second side and cover the pan until the cheese has melted. Risotto Cakes made with Quail-Leek Risotto (page 86) are an especially nice accompaniment to Quail Ragù (page 156).

Barley Risotto

RESEMBLING RISOTTO in taste and texture, *farroto,* which comes from Friuli, replaces rice with barley. Use pearled barley, from which the bran as well as the hull has been removed. Barley Risotto is especially good as a base for stews and sauced dishes. We like to serve it with Quail Ragù (page 156), Pork alla Romana (page 165), or Monkfish Osso Buco (page 138).

1 cup pearled barley
4 ounces shiitake mushrooms, cleaned, stemmed, and cut into small cubes (about 1½ cups)
4 cups Chicken Stock (see page 19)

Salt and freshly ground black pepper to taste
2 tablespoons freshly grated Parmigiano-Reggiano cheese

In a medium saucepan, combine the barley, half of the shiitakes, and the stock. Bring to a boil over high heat. Cover, reduce the heat to medium, and cook for 30 minutes.

Add the remaining mushrooms, salt, and pepper. Cook for about 10 minutes more, until the liquid is almost totally absorbed. Stir in the Parmesan and serve.

Yield = 6 servings
Fat per serving = 0.68 g.
Calories per serving = 151.7

Lemon Risotto

4 cups Chicken Stock (see page 19)

3 ounces yellow onion (about 1 small onion), chopped (about ½ cup)

2 tablespoons dry white wine or water

1¼ cups Vialone Nano, Carnaroli, or Arborio rice

2 tablespoons nonfat egg substitute

½ tablespoon finely grated lemon zest

¼ cup freshly squeezed lemon juice

Freshly ground black pepper to taste

2 tablespoons freshly grated Parmigiano-Reggiano cheese

Bring the chicken stock to a boil in a medium saucepan. Reduce the heat to maintain a simmer.

Combine the onion and wine or water in a large, heavy-bottomed pan. Stirring constantly, cook over medium heat for 5 to 6 minutes, until translucent. Add the rice. Cook and stir for 2 minutes more.

Slowly add 1½ cups of the stock, stirring vigorously over medium heat. When the stock has been mostly absorbed and small craters dot the surface, add another ½ cup. Stir and bring back to a simmer. Continue to add the remaining stock, ½ cup at a time, stirring after each addition. After the last addition, keep stirring until the liquid has been absorbed and the rice is creamy. Preparation of this risotto should take 18 to 20 minutes from the first addition of stock.

Meanwhile, combine the egg substitute, lemon zest, and lemon juice in a small bowl.

Stir the lemon mixture and the black pepper into the finished risotto. Serve 1 cup to each person, topping each serving with ½ tablespoon grated Parmesan.

Yield = 4 servings
Fat per serving = 0.72 g.
Calories per serving = 260.0

THIS CITRUS RISOTTO is almost as versatile as it is unusual. Our favorite way to serve it is with Skewered Lemon Turkey (page 155); it also makes a nice pairing for Turkey with Mushrooms, Zucchini, and Fennel (page 160). For a vegetarian entree, make Lemon Risotto with vegetable stock instead of with chicken stock and serve it with Lemon-Garlic Broccoli (page 189).

Roasted Yellow Pepper Risotto

7 ounces roasted yellow pepper (see Pantry)

4 cups Chicken Stock (see page 19)

6 ounces Vidalia onion (about 1 onion), chopped (about 1 cup)

1/4 cup water

1 1/2 cups Vialone Nano, Carnaroli, or Arborio rice

1 cup dry white wine

2 tablespoons freshly grated Pecorino Toscano cheese

1/8 teaspoon freshly ground black pepper

2 tablespoons chopped fresh flat-leaf parsley

Puree the roasted pepper in a food processor. Set aside.

Bring the Chicken Stock to a boil in a medium saucepan. Reduce the heat to maintain a simmer.

Preheat a large, heavy-bottomed pan over high heat. Add the onion and cook, stirring constantly, until translucent, about 1 minute. Add the water and cook 1 to 2 minutes, stirring, until all the water has been absorbed. Add the rice. Cook and stir until browned, about 2 minutes.

Reduce the heat to medium-low. Slowly add 1 1/2 cups of the stock, stirring vigorously. When the stock has been mostly absorbed and small craters dot the surface, add another 1 cup. Stir and bring back to a simmer. Stir in the wine. Add another 1/2 cup stock and the roasted pepper puree. Continue to add the remaining stock 1/2 cup at a time, stirring after each addition. After the last addition, keep stirring until the liquid has been absorbed and the rice is creamy. The total preparation should take 20 to 25 minutes from the first addition of stock.

Stir in the grated cheese, black pepper, and parsley. Serve a scant 1 cup to each person.

Yield = 6 servings
Fat per serving = 0.86 g.
Calories per serving = 255.3

Spinach Risotto

3 cups Chicken Stock (see page 19)

$1/3$ cup chopped purple (red) onion

2 tablespoons water

1 cup Vialone Nano, Carnaroli, or
   Arborio rice

1 clove garlic, peeled

One 10-ounce package frozen
   chopped spinach, thawed and
   squeezed dry (about $2/3$ cup)

$1/3$ cup dry white wine

2 tablespoons chopped fresh oregano

2 tablespoons freshly grated
   Parmigiano-Reggiano cheese

$1/2$ teaspoon freshly ground black
   pepper

Salt to taste

Bring the Chicken Stock to a boil in a medium saucepan. Reduce the heat to maintain a simmer.

Combine the onion and water in a large, heavy-bottomed pan. Stirring constantly, cook over medium heat for 7 to 8 minutes, until soft and translucent. Add the rice. Cook and stir for 3 minutes more.

Slowly add 1 cup of the stock, stirring vigorously over medium heat. Press in the garlic. When the stock has been mostly absorbed and small craters dot the surface, add another $1/2$ cup. Stir and bring back to a simmer. Continue to add the remaining stock $1/2$ cup at a time, stirring after each addition. Along with the last $1/2$ cup stock, add the spinach and wine. Keep stirring until the liquid has been absorbed and the rice is creamy. Total preparation should take 15 to 20 minutes from the first addition of stock.

Stir in the oregano, grated cheese, black pepper, and salt to taste. Serve 1 cup to each person.

Yield = 4 servings
Fat per serving = 0.66 g.
Calories per serving = 231.7

WE CALL FOR FROZEN spinach in this recipe for convenience. To use fresh spinach, rinse it and wilt it over high heat for 2 to 3 minutes with water still clinging to the leaves; squeeze out the excess liquid and chop the spinach. Spinach Risotto complements Tilapia Bundles with Tomato-Caper Sauce (page 146). Made with vegetable stock instead of chicken stock, it goes well with Cauliflower Italian Style (page 192).

Artichoke Risotto

Try ARTICHOKE Risotto as a first course before Chicken Piccata (page 163). Frozen artichoke hearts work perfectly well in this recipe, but you could, of course, use fresh artichoke hearts and bottoms, quartered, if you wish. Canned artichoke hearts should be rinsed and drained thoroughly before you use them.

5 cups Chicken Stock (see page 19)
4 ounces scallions (2 to 3 scallions), chopped (about $\frac{1}{3}$ cup)
4 large cloves garlic, minced
2 tablespoons water
1½ cups Vialone Nano, Carnaroli, or Arborio rice

One 10-ounce package frozen artichoke hearts, thawed and drained
¼ cup chopped fresh flat-leaf parsley
Salt and freshly ground black pepper to taste
1½ tablespoons freshly grated Parmigiano-Reggiano cheese

In a medium saucepan, bring the Chicken Stock to a boil. Adjust the heat to maintain a simmer.

Combine the scallions, garlic, and water in a large, heavy-bottomed pan. Cook for 4 minutes over medium-low heat, stirring constantly. Add the rice and continue to cook and stir for another 3 minutes.

Slowly add 1 cup of the hot stock, stirring vigorously, and allow it to come back to a simmer. When the stock has been almost all absorbed and small craters dot the surface, stir in another ½ cup and bring back to a simmer. Continue to add another 2½ cups of the stock, ½ cup at a time. Stir in the artichokes and parsley, then another ½ cup stock. When this addition has been absorbed, stir in the remaining ½ cup. Continue to stir until all the stock has been absorbed and the rice is creamy. Stir in the salt, pepper, and Parmesan. Preparation of this risotto should take about 30 minutes from the first addition of stock. Serve ¾ cup to each person.

Yield = 6 servings
Fat per serving = 0.66 g.
Calories per serving = 212.8

Mushroom Risotto

5 cups Chicken Stock (see page 19)

4 ounces yellow onion (about 1 small onion), chopped (about ¾ cup)

1½ cups Vialone Nano, Carnaroli, or Arborio rice

1 cup dry white wine

6 ounces cremini mushrooms, roughly chopped (about 3 cups)

8 ounces white button mushrooms, roughly chopped (about 3 cups)

Freshly ground black pepper to taste

1 tablespoon freshly grated Pecorino Romano cheese

In a medium saucepan, bring the Chicken Stock to a boil, then adjust the heat to maintain a constant simmer.

In a Dutch oven, sauté the onion over medium heat until translucent, about 3 minutes. Add the rice and cook for about 3 minutes more, until lightly toasted, stirring constantly. Raise the heat to medium-high and add the wine. Stir in the mushrooms and cook until the liquid in the pan has been mostly absorbed, 1 to 2 minutes.

Vigorously stir in 1½ cups of the hot stock and continue to cook for several minutes over medium-high heat, until it has been absorbed and small craters dot the surface. Add the remaining stock in ½ cup increments, stirring after each addition and then waiting for the stock to be absorbed. Stir until the risotto is creamy and tender, then stir in the black pepper and cheese. Preparation of this risotto should take 25 to 30 minutes from the first addition of stock. Serve ¾ cup risotto to each person.

Yield = 6 servings
Fat per serving = 0.76 g.
Calories per serving = 251.4

MUSHROOM RISOTTO pairs nicely with Veal Spiedini (page 154) to make a satisfying meal. It also accents Pork alla Romana (page 165) and Turkey alla Cacciatora (page 162). The brown cremini mushrooms boost the flavor of the white mushrooms; for incrementally stronger mushroom taste, substitute portobellos, use all creminis, or, for the strongest flavor of all, use all portobellos.

Quail-Leek Risotto

THIS UNIQUE RISOTTO takes a bit longer than most to prepare, since the stock is made from scratch at the start of the recipe, but it is well worth the effort. It makes an elegant prelude to Quail Ragù (page 156) and could easily stand on its own as a main dish for 4. For a less exotic rendition, replace the quail stock and quail meat with chicken stock and meat. You could also substitute leftover turkey meat, pressing the carcass into service to make turkey stock.

3 quails (about 12 ounces total)
½ carrot
1 small stalk celery
¼ onion
3 cloves garlic, peeled
1 sprig thyme
1 sprig flat-leaf parsley plus 1½ tablespoons chopped
1 bay leaf
4 cups water
About 1½ cups Chicken Stock (see page 19)

1 cup dry white wine
1 cup sliced leek (white and light green parts only)
1½ cups Vialone Nano, Carnaroli, or Arborio rice
½ teaspoon chopped fresh rosemary
Salt and freshly ground black pepper to taste
1 tablespoon plus 1 teaspoon freshly grated Parmigiano-Reggiano cheese

Preheat the oven to 450 degrees.

Remove the legs, wings, skin, and bones from the quails and place them on a baking sheet. Dice and reserve the breast meat. (You should have about ⅔ cup.)

Add the carrot, celery, onion, and garlic to the pan with the quail parts. Roast on the bottom of the oven for 11 to 12 minutes, until well browned. Remove to a large saucepan and add the sprigs of thyme and parsley and the bay leaf. Add the water and bring to a boil. Simmer, uncovered, for about 35 minutes over medium heat.

Suspend a strainer over a large glass measuring cup and strain in the quail stock. Refrigerate, uncovered, for 45 to 60 minutes. With a spoon, skim off the fat that has coagulated on top. Add as much of the Chicken Stock as you need to bring the total volume to 4 cups.

In a medium saucepan, bring the quail-chicken stock to a boil over medium heat. Add the wine and adjust the heat to maintain a constant simmer.

In a large, heavy-bottomed pan, sauté the leek over medium heat for about 5 minutes, until soft. Add the rice and continue to cook and stir for 2 minutes. Slowly add $1\frac{1}{2}$ cups of hot stock, stirring vigorously. When the liquid has been absorbed and craters begin to dot the surface, add the reserved quail breast meat and $1\frac{1}{2}$ cups more of the stock. Stir and bring back to a simmer.

Add the rest of the stock, $\frac{1}{2}$ cup at a time, waiting for the stock to be absorbed between additions and stirring after each. With the last $\frac{1}{2}$ cup, stir in the chopped parsley and rosemary. Continue to stir until the rice is tender. Stir in the salt, black pepper, and Parmesan before serving. Preparation of this risotto should take about 25 minutes from the first addition of stock. Serve $\frac{3}{4}$ cup to each person.

Yield = 6 servings
Fat per serving = 0.82 g.
Calories per serving = 241.0

Risotto al Barolo

This vibrant risotto derives its pretty ruby-red hue from red wine—originally Barolo, but any fairly good dry red wine will suffice. We dispense with the traditional inclusion of beef marrow because of the fat content, but finish with a flourish of hearty Pecorino Romano cheese. The risotto makes a nice accompaniment to meat dishes and to such full-flavored fish as grilled tuna.

4$\frac{1}{3}$ cups Chicken Stock (see page 19)
3 ounces yellow onion (about 1 small onion), finely chopped (about $\frac{1}{2}$ cup)
2 tablespoons water
1$\frac{1}{2}$ cups Vialone Nano, Carnaroli, or Arborio rice

$\frac{2}{3}$ cup dry red wine
Freshly ground black pepper to taste
2 tablespoons freshly grated Pecorino Romano cheese

In a medium saucepan, bring the Chicken Stock to a boil. Adjust the heat to maintain a simmer.

Preheat a large, heavy-bottomed pan over medium heat. Add the onion and water. Cook for about 2 minutes, stirring constantly, until the water has been absorbed and the onion is translucent. Add the rice and continue to cook and stir for another 4 minutes.

Slowly add 1$\frac{1}{2}$ cups of the hot stock, stirring vigorously over medium heat, and allow it to come to a simmer. When the stock has been almost all absorbed and small craters dot the surface, stir in another 1 cup and bring back to a simmer. Stir in the wine. Continue to add the remaining stock $\frac{1}{2}$ cup at a time. Continue to stir until all the stock has been absorbed and the rice is creamy. Stir in the pepper and cheese. Preparation of this risotto should take about 20 minutes from the first addition of stock. Serve $\frac{3}{4}$ cup to each person.

Yield = 6 servings
Fat per serving = 0.77 g.
Calories per serving = 235.0

Dried Pasta

(Pasta Secca)

Tomatoes, Potatoes, and Scallops on Penne ⌒ Broccoli and Shells ⌒ Pasta with Shrimp ⌒ Rapini and Orecchiette ⌒ Bucatini alla Carbonara ⌒ Saffron Pasta with Mussels ⌒ Fusilli with Roasted Zucchini ⌒ Pasta with Portobello Mushroom and Mixed Vegetable Sauce ⌒ Scallops with Linguine ⌒ Squash and Mixed Mushroom Lasagne ⌒ Rigatoni with Artichokes, Fava Beans, and Arugula

6. Dried Pasta

(Pasta Secca)

The Italians truly work magic with pasta. They appreciate pasta in all shapes, sizes, and textures and know instinctively how to pair it with a sauce of just the right flavor and consistency.

Pasta fresca, the delicate fresh pasta made at home with soft wheat and eggs, and *pasta secca*, the sturdier commercial product manufactured from hard wheat and water, are viewed as equal, if different, siblings. The current notion that fresh pasta (especially the "fresh" pasta that is produced commercially with enough preservatives to give it a shelf life of months) is somehow superior to dried pasta is strictly an American affectation.

During the past year or two, several brands of dried pasta that are low in fat have come onto the market, including some high-quality imports from Italy. Look for a product that has no more than 0.5 gram of fat for every 2 ounces. The other major adaptation for cooking pasta in the fat-free kitchen is to resist the urge to reach for the bottle of olive oil when starting a sauce; learn to work instead with wine or stock.

Our sampling of dried pasta selections runs the gamut from little shaped pastas tossed with bits of broccoli in a simple garlic-infused stock or with roasted zucchini matchsticks in a silky nonfat cream sauce, to delicate strands paired with scallops or calamari in light tomato sauce, to versatile penne served with saffron and mussels or in a meaty portobello-based sauce. Servings are the size of a typical Italian first course, or about that of a lunch or light supper portion. A dish that serves 6 as a pasta course would serve 4 nicely as a typical American entree, and a dish that serves 4 would make a very substantial meal for 2.

To cook pasta, fill a large, wide-mouthed pot with cold water and bring to a boil. (The kind with a basket insert designed specifically for cooking pasta makes draining easier.) Salt as directed, put in the pasta, carefully pushing the strands into the water without breaking them, and cook, maintaining a boil and stirring occasionally.

The pasta is done when *al dente,* or resistant "to the tooth," which usually takes 8 to 10 minutes for spaghetti or penne, but is better determined by sampling a strand than by following the suggested cooking time on the package. Remember that the pasta will continue to cook after you take the pot off the heat, so err on the side of undercooking by a minute or two. Once the pasta is cooked, don't dawdle. Drain it quickly (made easier by using an insert or a pasta fork), leaving a little water clinging to the pasta for added moisture. Toss it immediately in the heated sauce, add cheese if desired, and serve it in warmed pasta bowls or on a warmed platter.

To warm the platter easily and speed things up a bit, place it over the pasta pot for the first minute or two of cooking.

Tomatoes, Potatoes, and Scallops on Penne

2 cloves garlic, chopped

$\frac{1}{8}$ teaspoon crushed red pepper flakes

8 ounces baking potato (about 1 potato), peeled and cut into $\frac{1}{4}$-inch cubes (about 1 cup)

1 pound tomatoes (about 2 tomatoes), peeled, seeded, and chopped (about $1\frac{1}{2}$ cups), or $1\frac{1}{2}$ cups cut-up boxed or canned tomatoes with their juice

4 ounces white button mushrooms, cleaned, trimmed, and chopped

Salt to taste

5 ounces penne

8 ounces bay scallops

In a medium nonstick saucepan, combine the garlic and crushed red pepper over medium heat. Cook until the garlic is very aromatic, stirring frequently, about 2 minutes. Stir in the potato, tomatoes, and mushrooms. Cover and cook for about 30 minutes, until the potato is soft.

Meanwhile, bring a large saucepan of water to a boil over high heat. Salt, add the penne, and cook until tender. Drain and put in a large serving bowl.

Add the scallops to the potato mixture. Cover and cook for about 5 minutes, until the scallops turn opaque. Combine with the penne, add salt to taste, and toss. Serve about $1\frac{1}{4}$ cups to each person.

Yield = 4 servings
Fat per serving = 0.82 g.
Calories per serving = 251.3

THE ITALIANS VIEW potatoes as just another vegetable rather than as a starch, and thus are much more apt to serve them with pasta than we are. To the American palate, the combination makes for a very filling dish. Take care not to overcook the tiny bay scallops, which are done in a matter of minutes. An alternative way of cooking them, which sears and browns them a little more, is to push the sauce to one side of the pan with a wooden spoon, creating a space in which to sauté the scallops before combining them with the tomato-and-potato mixture.

Broccoli and Shells

THE CLASSIC combination of broccoli and pasta is a perfect summer meal. It's light—especially in our rendition, which is made with stock instead of oil—and quick to prepare, so you won't have to labor long in a hot kitchen. Any other small shaped pasta with crevices to which little bits of broccoli and sauce can cling, such as lumachelle, cavatelli, or orecchiette, could be substituted for the shells. We like the heat that comes from tossing a hearty dash of red pepper flakes into the finished dish, but those with less tolerance for spice can easily dispense with this addition.

To cook the broccoli on the stove instead of in the microwave, bring a pot of water to a boil, lightly salt, and cook the broccoli until it is bright green and crisp-tender, 4 to 5 minutes. Continue with the recipe as directed.

8 ounces broccoli florets (about 4 cups)
2 tablespoons water
4 cloves garlic, chopped
1½ cups Chicken or Vegetable Stock (see pages 19 and 20)
½ teaspoon salt plus additional to taste

8 ounces conchigliette (small shells)
Freshly ground black pepper to taste
2 teaspoons freshly grated Parmigiano-Reggiano cheese
Up to ½ teaspoon crushed red pepper flakes (optional)

Combine the broccoli and the 2 tablespoons water in a microwave-safe container, cover, and microwave at full power until crisp-tender, about 2 minutes. Chop and set aside.

Bring a large saucepan of water to a boil over high heat.

Meanwhile, combine the garlic and ¼ cup of the stock in a medium saucepan over medium heat. Cook just until the stock begins to steam and the garlic begins to become aromatic, less than a minute. Add the cooked broccoli and the remaining 1¼ cups stock. Stir to combine and continue to cook for about 10 minutes, until the broccoli can be broken up with the back of a wooden spoon.

When the water has come to a boil, add the ½ teaspoon salt and the shells. Cook over high heat until tender. Drain and transfer the shells to a bowl. Add the broccoli and salt and black pepper to taste. Toss with the Parmesan and, if desired, the red pepper flakes.

Serve about 1 cup to each person.

Yield = 4 servings
Fat per serving = 0.76 g.
Calories per serving = 233.5

Pasta with Shrimp

6 ounces yellow onion (about 1 onion), diced (about 1 generous cup)

¼ cup water

2 tablespoons chopped garlic (6 to 8 cloves)

¼ cup chopped fresh flat-leaf parsley

¼ cup dry white wine

1½ cups cut-up boxed or canned tomatoes with their juice

Pinch of crushed red pepper flakes

6 ounces dried spaghettini or vermicelli

8 ounces shelled medium shrimp, halved

Salt to taste

SOMETIMES WE prepare this recipe with squid instead of shrimp, for variety. Whichever seafood you choose, use spaghettini or vermicelli and finish with a touch of red pepper flakes.

Preheat a large nonstick skillet over medium heat. Add the onion and the ¼ cup water. Cook for 2 to 3 minutes, stirring constantly, until the water has evaporated and the onion has just begun to color. Add the garlic and cook for a few seconds more, until it begins to become aromatic. Stir in the parsley and wine and cook for about 2 minutes more. Add the tomatoes and crushed red pepper. Cook for about 15 minutes to form a thick sauce.

Meanwhile, bring a large pot of water to a boil over high heat. Salt, add the pasta, and cook until *al dente*. Drain and put into a serving bowl.

Add the shrimp to the tomato sauce and cook, stirring, until the shrimp turn pink, 1 to 2 minutes. Pour the sauce over the pasta, add more salt to taste, and toss to coat. Serve immediately.

Yield = 4 servings
Fat per serving = 1.00 g.
Calories per serving = 283.5

ITALIANS LOVE *RAPINI* or broccoli raab, a considerably more pungent relative of broccoli that's just beginning to catch on enough in this country to be readily available in supermarkets. In this recipe, its inherent bitterness is juxtaposed with a hint of sweetness from evaporated milk and brandy in our light rendition of an Italian cream sauce. We pair it with orecchiette, the little pasta shaped like ears.

Rapini and Orecchiette

1 pound rapini
6 ounces white onion (about 1 onion), coarsely chopped (about 1 cup)
1/4 cup water
1/4 cup brandy or cognac
1/2 cup evaporated skim milk

1/4 teaspoon salt
8 ounces orecchiette
1/2 teaspoon freshly ground black pepper
1 teaspoon freshly grated Parmigiano-Reggiano cheese

Set a large pot of water to boil.

Remove and discard the rapini's thick, woody stems. Rinse thoroughly in a sink filled with water. Roughly chop the rapini into 1-inch pieces (about 6 cups).

Preheat a large nonstick skillet over high heat. Add the onion and cook, stirring, until it is just beginning to turn brown, about 1 minute. Reduce the heat to medium-low and add the 1/4 cup water. Cover and cook until the onion is limp and dry, 1 to 2 minutes. Remove the cover and add the brandy. Stirring constantly, cook until the brandy has been absorbed, about 30 seconds. Add the evaporated milk and the rapini. Cover and cook for about 8 minutes, until the rapini is tender. Remove from the heat.

Meanwhile, salt the pot of boiling water and add the orecchiette. Cook until tender. Drain the pasta and add it to the rapini mixture. Add the black pepper and Parmesan. Return to medium-low heat. Cook, tossing, until the sauce has been absorbed.

Serve about 1 1/4 cups to each person.

Yield = 4 servings
Fat per serving = 0.95 g.
Calories per serving = 281.5

Bucatini alla Carbonara

¾ cup nonfat liquid egg substitute

¼ cup chopped fresh flat-leaf parsley

1 teaspoon freshly ground black pepper

1 tablespoon freshly grated Parmigiano-Reggiano cheese

2 slices turkey bacon, cut into ¼-inch cubes

2 tablespoons water

3 or 4 cloves garlic, smashed and peeled

½ cup dry white wine

Salt to taste

8 ounces bucatini

In a large bowl, combine the egg substitute, parsley, black pepper, and Parmesan. Mix and set aside.

Set a large saucepan of water to boil over high heat.

Put the bacon, the 1 tablespoon water, and the garlic into a large nonstick skillet. Cook over medium heat for about 10 minutes, stirring occasionally, until the bacon is lightly browned. Add the wine and cook until it is reduced by half, about 2 minutes. Remove the pan from the heat and discard the garlic.

Meanwhile, add salt and the bucatini to the boiling water. Cook until tender.

Drain the pasta and add it to the bowl with the egg substitute mixture. Stir well to coat. Add to the skillet, return the skillet to the heat, and cook and toss over low heat until warmed through. Add more salt to taste. Serve about 1 cup to each person.

Yield = 4 servings
Fat per serving = 0.94 g.
Calories per serving = 271.9

OUR TAKE ON THE classic Roman preparation is rich and creamy, though we have taken a few liberties with the original. Using a pasteurized egg substitute made from egg whites accomplishes two ends—it rids the dish of the fatty egg yolk, and it removes the danger of consuming barely cooked egg. (In the original version, hot pasta is tossed in a raw egg-yolk mixture just long enough to cook the egg lightly.) We also replace sautéed pancetta with crisp-cooked, lean turkey bacon.

Although the dish is usually prepared with spaghetti, we rather like using the tubular bucatini, so the sauce coats the pasta on the inside as well as the outside. This sauce also works well with such flat, thick noodles as fettuccine, if you want to try it with Homemade Pasta (page 111). Despite the fact that you no longer need to cook the egg with the heat of the pasta, this is best served very warm.

Saffron Pasta with Mussels

SAFFRON IS expensive, but exquisite and used very sparingly—a smidgeon lends a world of character. Buy saffron threads rather than powder; the threads stay fresher, and on occasion the powder has been cut with ground turmeric by an avaricious spice merchant. We use the large variety of frozen, partially cooked green-lip mussels for convenience and cut them into thirds; if you use blue mussels, steam them open and use them whole. Whole bay scallops or quartered sea scallops make a nice variation.

To prepare the leek, cut the green leaves off but leave the root end intact. Starting 1/4 to 1/2 inch above the root end, slice the leek down the middle. Fan it open under cold running water to remove all residual grit, then cut it crosswise into thin half-moons. Discard the root end.

1/4 teaspoon salt

6 ounces penne

6 ounces leek (about 1 large leek), trimmed of all green portions, cleaned, and thinly sliced (see sidebar)

1/2 cup dry white wine

1 clove garlic, minced

1 cup clam juice

Pinch of saffron

12 ounces green-lip mussels (about 9 large mussels), shelled and cut in thirds

2 tablespoons chopped fresh flat-leaf parsley

1/2 teaspoon lemon zest

Bring a large saucepan of water to a boil over high heat. Salt, add the penne, and cook until tender. Drain.

Preheat a large nonstick skillet over medium-high heat. Add the leek and wine and cook for about 3 minutes, stirring constantly, until the wine has evaporated and the leek is very soft. Add the garlic. Cook and stir for 1 minute. Add the clam juice and cook for about 5 minutes more, until the liquid is reduced by about half.

Stir in the saffron, then the mussels. Cook for about 3 minutes to heat through. Add the penne, raise the heat to high, and cook for about 3 minutes more, until the pasta has turned saffron-yellow.

Garnish with the parsley and lemon zest. Serve a generous 3/4 cup to each person.

Yield = 6 servings
Fat per serving = 0.71 g.
Calories per serving = 146.6

Fusilli with Roasted Zucchini

1 pound zucchini (about 2 large
   zucchini)

Olive oil cooking spray

¼ cup chopped fresh basil

2 tablespoons nonfat liquid egg
   substitute

1 tablespoon freshly grated
   Parmigiano-Reggiano cheese

Salt to taste

8 ounces fusilli

½ cup skim milk

1 tablespoon all-purpose flour

Freshly ground black pepper to taste

A SILKY YET SVELTE cream sauce coats the corkscrew twists of the fusilli in this dish. Cutting the zucchini into sticks before roasting it facilitates all-round browning and creates a crispiness that provides a nice textural contrast to the slight chewiness of the pasta.

Preheat the oven to 400 degrees.

Cut the zucchini lengthwise into thin strips and then cut the strips cross-wise into thirds, creating 1½-by-1-inch sticks. In a bowl, spray the sticks lightly with the olive oil while tossing to coat them thoroughly. Place them on a baking sheet and roast for 20 minutes, until well browned, tossing after 10 minutes.

In a small bowl, mix together the basil, egg substitute, and Parmesan cheese. Set aside.

Bring a large saucepan of water to a boil over high heat. Salt, add the fusilli, and cook until tender.

Meanwhile, combine the skim milk and flour in a skillet. Stirring occasionally, cook over medium-low heat just until steaming, 3 to 5 minutes.

Drain the fusilli and return it to the saucepan. Add the milk mixture, the zucchini, and the egg-substitute-and-cheese mixture. Cook briefly until the cheese has melted and the sauce is heated through and creamy. Add black pepper and additional salt to taste.

Serve about 1¼ cups to each person.

Yield = 4 servings
Fat per serving = 0.96 g.
Calories per serving = 252.1

Pasta with Portobello Mushroom and Mixed Vegetable Sauce

This is a wonderfully flavorful and filling dish that could easily serve as a vegetarian meal—just substitute 1 cup vegetable broth or bouillon for the beef soup base and water. The hearty sauce is brimming with meaty portobello mushrooms and big chunks of other vegetables. For this recipe, you'll want to use a sturdy tubular pasta such as penne or rigatoni.

8 ounces yellow onion (about 1 onion), peeled and cut into chunks

4 ounces carrot (about 1 carrot), peeled and cut into chunks

2 ounces celery (about 1 stalk), trimmed and cut into chunks

1 pound portobello mushrooms, cleaned

1/2 cup dry white wine

1 1/2 cups cut-up boxed or canned tomatoes with their juice

1/2 tablespoon instant beef soup base

1 cup water

1/2 teaspoon salt plus additional to taste

12 ounces penne or rigatoni

Freshly ground black pepper to taste

1/2 tablespoon freshly grated Parmigiano-Reggiano cheese

Combine the onion, carrot, celery, and mushrooms in the bowl of a food processor and process to a fine chop. Transfer the chopped vegetables to a large nonstick skillet and add the wine. Cook over medium heat for about 20 minutes, stirring occasionally, until the vegetables are very soft. Raise the heat to medium-high and cook until all the liquid has evaporated, 5 to 10 minutes. Stir in the tomatoes, the beef soup base, and the 1 cup water. Allow to boil for 8 to 10 minutes, stirring periodically, until the mixture is thick and dry.

Meanwhile, bring a large saucepan of water to a boil over high heat. Add the 1/2 teaspoon salt and the pasta. Cook until tender. Drain.

Combine the pasta and sauce. Add salt and pepper to taste. Add the Parmesan and toss to coat. Serve about 1 1/3 cups to each person.

Yield = 6 servings
Fat per serving = 1.00 g.
Calories per serving = 272.8

Scallops with Linguine

3 cloves garlic, chopped

¼ teaspoon crushed red pepper flakes

2 tablespoons water

2½ cups cut-up boxed or canned tomatoes with their juice, or 1½ pounds tomatoes (2 to 3 tomatoes), peeled, seeded, and chopped (about 2½ cups)

1 cup white wine

1 cup packed fresh basil leaves, chopped

1 teaspoon salt plus additional to taste

12 ounces dried linguine

12 ounces bay scallops

Set a large pot of water to boil over high heat.

Preheat a large nonstick skillet over medium heat. Add the garlic, crushed red pepper, and the 2 tablespoons water. Cook for about 2 minutes, stirring constantly, until most of the water has evaporated and the garlic is aromatic. Add the tomatoes and wine. Cover and cook for about 5 minutes, until the tomatoes have softened. Uncover, stir in the basil, and cook for about 8 minutes more, stirring frequently, until the tomatoes have broken down and thickened into a sauce.

When the pot of water is boiling, add the 1 teaspoon salt and the linguine. Cook until *al dente*.

Meanwhile, raise the heat under the skillet to high and push the tomato sauce to one side of the pan with a wooden spoon. Add the scallops to the other side of the pan and sauté for 1 minute. Mix the scallops and sauce and continue to cook for up to 1 minute more, stirring, until the scallops have turned opaque. Remove from the heat.

Drain the pasta, allowing some water to cling to the strands, and add it to the skillet with the sauce. Add additional salt to taste, toss, and serve.

Yield = 6 servings
Fat per serving = 0.91 g.
Calories per serving = 324.1

RIBBONS OF LINGUINE go well with little bay scallops dressed in a light tomato sauce. You could also use sea scallops, quartered. The quality of bay scallops is less consistent than that of sea scallops, but when they're in their prime, in the fall, they are incomparable—sweeter and tenderer than the larger variety.

Timing is important at the end of preparing this dish. Remove the pan from the heat after the scallops have been seared so they don't overcook, quickly drain the pasta, toss, and serve piping hot.

Squash and Mixed Mushroom Lasagne

THIS VERSATILE vegetarian dish can be a first course for 6, a hearty main dish for 4, or a side dish for 8. The vegetables take a little effort to prepare, but we compensate by using a high-quality prepared sauce and no-boil lasagne noodles, which are now carried by most supermarkets. The brand stocked by our local market, which is imported from Italy, even comes in a little aluminum tray in which you can bake the lasagne if you wish. Made with semolina and no egg, it has half the fat of traditional lasagne noodles. The thin noodles break easily to fit your casserole and soften readily from the moisture of the sauce.

8 sun-dried tomatoes
1/4 cup boiling water
1 cup skim-milk ricotta cheese
2 tablespoons nonfat liquid egg substitute
2 tablespoons chopped fresh flat-leaf parsley
Freshly ground black pepper to taste
3 scallions, trimmed and chopped (about 1/4 cup)
4 ounces carrot (about 1 carrot), peeled and chopped (about 1/2 cup)
2 cloves garlic, minced
8 ounces white button mushrooms, sliced (about 3 cups)

6 ounces portobello mushrooms (about 2 mushrooms), cut into 1/2-inch pieces (about 3 cups)
1 tablespoon chopped fresh rosemary
1 1/2 cups high-quality prepared Italian tomato sauce
Salt and freshly ground black pepper to taste
Olive oil cooking spray
8 ounces no-boil lasagne noodles
12 ounces butternut squash (about 1 small squash), peeled, quartered, and thinly sliced (about 2 cups)
1 tablespoon freshly grated Parmigiano-Reggiano cheese

Preheat the oven to 400 degrees.

Combine the sun-dried tomatoes and boiling water in a bowl and let stand for 10 minutes so the tomatoes can reconstitute. Drain and reserve the liquid. Chop the tomatoes (about 1/4 cup).

In a bowl, mix together the ricotta cheese, egg substitute, parsley, and black pepper. Set aside.

Preheat a large nonstick skillet over medium-high heat. Add the scallions and cook until just beginning to brown, about 1 minute. Add the carrot and garlic and stir 2 or 3 times. Add the mushrooms and the reserved tomato steeping liquid. Cook for about 5 minutes, until the mixture is dry. Stir in the reconstituted tomatoes and the rosemary, then 1 cup of the tomato sauce.

Cook for about 2 minutes more, until the mixture thickens slightly. Remove from the heat and add salt and pepper to taste.

Coat a 7-by-11-inch baking dish lightly with the olive oil spray. Spread 2 tablespoons of the remaining tomato sauce over the bottom of the pan. Layer the noodles over the sauce and spread with half of the mushroom mixture (about 1½ cups). Add a second layer of noodles. Top with all the squash, additional salt and pepper if desired, and all of the ricotta cheese mixture. Add a third layer of noodles, then the remaining mushroom mixture. Add the last layer of noodles and top with the remaining 6 tablespoons tomato sauce and the Parmesan cheese.

Spray a sheet of aluminum foil on one side with the olive oil and cover the baking dish with the foil, oiled side down. Bake for 45 minutes.

Remove from the oven and let cool for 10 minutes before serving.

Yield = 8 servings
Fat per serving = 0.94 g.
Calories per serving = 187.2

Rigatoni with Artichokes, Fava Beans, and Arugula

Some of the prettiest and most flavorful vegetables and greens—artichokes, fava beans, and arugula—are grouped in this lovely dish, which makes a stunning, rather rustic presentation. The delicate sauce is derived from the pasta cooking liquid flavored with just a hint of sun-dried tomato paste.

Select small, tender artichokes. You could use frozen artichoke hearts to save time and effort, but that would be a shame. The long, thin artichoke segments are much more attractive and provide an intriguing mix of textures that can't be captured by the hearts alone. If you prefer your artichokes on the soft side rather than with a bit of crunch, microwave them at full power for about 3 minutes before roasting.

1 pound small, tender artichokes (2 to 3 artichokes)
2 tablespoons freshly squeezed lemon juice
4 cups water
Olive oil cooking spray
3/4 teaspoon salt
3/4 pound fava beans, shelled

6 ounces rigatoni
1 tablespoon sun-dried tomato paste
3 ounces arugula, stemmed (about 2 cups)
1 tablespoon freshly grated Parmigiano-Reggiano cheese
1/8 teaspoon crushed red pepper flakes

Preheat the broiler.

Stem the artichokes just below the smallest leaves at the bottom, leaving just a bit of stem intact. Trim about 1/2 inch of the leaves from the top. Remove the tough, dark green outer leaves to expose the tender, pale green leaves that are more tightly closed around the chokes. Quarter each artichoke lengthwise and remove the choke and the small, spiny, purple-tipped leaves. Cut each quarter in half again lengthwise to form thin triangular sections. Combine the lemon juice and 2 cups of the water and dip the artichokes into the mixture.

Spray a broiler pan lightly to coat it with the olive oil. Lay the triangular artichoke segments on their backs on the pan and position 5 inches from the heat source. Broil for 4 minutes, turn the segments onto one side, and broil for 2 minutes more. Turn again and broil for another minute or two on the other side. Remove from the oven and set aside.

Bring the remaining 2 cups of water to a boil in a medium saucepan over high heat. Add 1/4 teaspoon of the salt and the fava beans. Cook for 30 seconds, drain, and rinse under cold water. Peel the beans.

Meanwhile, bring a large pot of water to a boil. Add the remaining 1/2 teaspoon salt and the rigatoni. Cook until tender. Drain the rigatoni, reserving

3 tablespoons of the cooking liquid, and return the pasta to the pot. In a small bowl, mix together the reserved cooking liquid and the tomato paste. Add the mixture to the pasta, along with the artichokes, fava beans, and arugula. Add the Parmesan and red pepper flakes and toss to coat.

Serve about 1¼ cups to each person.

Yield = 4 servings
Fat per serving = 0.96 g.
Calories per serving = 213.7

Fresh Pasta

(Pasta Fresca)

Homemade Pasta ∽ Shrimp and Zucchini Agnolotti ∽
Ricotta and Basil Tortellini ∽ Spinach Pasta ∽ Spinach
Fettucine with Baccalà and Tomato ∽ Roasted Tomato
Ravioli ∽ Carrot Pasta ∽ Homemade Gnocchi ∽
Pumpkin Gnocchi

7. *Fresh Pasta*

(Pasta Fresca)

There's nothing wrong with commercial pasta; manufacturers have been making perfectly fine dried pastas for years, good enough to please even the finicky Italians. However, the concept of commercially prepared "fresh" pasta is a dubious one at best. We believe that if you want fresh pasta, you should get fresh pasta—homemade, that is. Besides, it is almost impossible to find commercial fresh pasta prepared without fatty egg yolks.

In this chapter we provide straightforward directions for making fat-free egg pasta using an egg-white-based egg substitute, as well as for making carrot pasta and spinach pasta. Any of the varieties can simply be cut into strands (fettucine is probably the most versatile width of noodle) or fashioned into squares or circles for making tortellini, ravioli, or agnolotti. The dough can be made in advance and stored in the refrigerator for 3 to 5 days or in the freezer for up to a month.

To roll out the dough: Using a pasta machine is by far the easiest and most foolproof method of rolling and cutting for all but the most experienced cooks, and the modest investment in a hand-cranked model is easily justifiable.

Flour the rollers of the pasta machine. Cut the dough into 6 pieces, flour it all over, and flatten it. Put the first piece through the largest opening on the pasta machine 3 times, folding it in half after each time through. Then put it through each successively smaller opening until it goes through the smallest. Repeat the process for the remaining pieces of dough.

You can also proceed by hand, rolling the dough out into a rectangular shape about 1/8 inch thick.

To cut fettucine noodles: Put each of the thin sheets of rolled dough through the wide cutters on the pasta machine. Hang and dry the strands for 10 to 20 minutes.

To cut strands by hand, fold the rolled dough in half crosswise, then again

twice more so that it is folded in eighths. Cut it into ¼-inch strips, unfold the strips, and hang them up to dry.

To cook fresh fettucine: Follow the directions for cooking dried pasta (page 91) but reduce the cooking time. Whereas dried pasta takes 8 to 10 minutes, fresh takes only 3 to 5 minutes.

To cut pasta circles: Using a 3-inch round cookie cutter or a glass, cut 32 circles out of the thin sheets of rolled dough, gathering and rerolling the dough scraps as necessary.

To cut pasta squares: Cut thirty-two 3-inch squares out of the thin sheets of rolled dough, gathering and rerolling the dough scraps as necessary.

Homemade Pasta

2 cups all-purpose flour   1 cup nonfat liquid egg substitute

Put the flour into the bowl of a food processor. Pulse while drizzling the egg substitute through the feed tube.

Turn the soft ball of dough out onto a floured board and knead a few times into a single ball that is glossy and elastic. Enclose the ball in plastic wrap and set aside for 30 minutes.

Roll out and cut the dough into fettucine according to the directions on page 109.

Yield = 6 servings, or enough dough for 32 pasta circles or squares
Fat per serving = 0.33 g.
Calories per serving = 146.7

BY MAKING FRESH pasta at home, you not only do without the preservatives that give commercial egg pasta its shelf life, but you can use egg substitute made from egg whites to strip the pasta of superfluous fat as well. Look in your supermarket's freezer compartment for a brand of egg substitute made with only egg whites and a little coloring to restore the luster normally lent by fatty egg yolks—no other additives or oil.

We recommend making a supply of pasta to keep on hand in the freezer; the dough freezes well for up to a month. Try it with Meat Sauce (page 126), Raw Tomato Sauce (page 130), Spicy Roasted Garlic and Eggplant Sauce (page 125), or Almost Leslie's Garlic-Parsley Sauce (page 133).

Shrimp and Zucchini Agnolotti

3 ounces zucchini, cut into $\frac{1}{4}$-inch cubes

1 medium carrot, peeled and cut into $\frac{1}{4}$-inch cubes

1 stalk celery, trimmed and cut into $\frac{1}{4}$-inch cubes

1 tablespoon finely diced red bell pepper

1 scallion, finely chopped (about 1 tablespoon)

1 tablespoon chopped arugula

Thirty-two 3-inch pasta circles (see page 111 for the dough, page 110 for cutting directions), or round wonton wrappers

16 medium shrimp (about 8 ounces), peeled, deveined, and halved lengthwise

$\frac{1}{4}$ cup nonfat liquid egg substitute

In a bowl, mix together the zucchini, carrot, celery, bell pepper, scallion, and arugula for the filling.

To assemble, mound $\frac{1}{2}$ tablespoon of the vegetable mixture and half a shrimp on one side of each pasta circle. Paint the outer rim with egg substitute. Fold the empty side over the filling and crimp to seal.

To cook the agnolotti, fill a large saucepan about $\frac{2}{3}$ full of water, salt, and bring to a boil. Add the agnolotti to the boiling water and cook over medium-high heat for 5 minutes. Remove with a slotted spoon to a colander to drain. Serve 8 agnolotti to each person.

Yield = 4 servings
Fat per serving = 0.84 g.
Calories per serving = 291.9

Ricotta and Basil Tortellini

1 cup skim-milk ricotta cheese
2 egg whites
2 tablespoons finely chopped sun-
    dried tomato
1 tablespoon chopped fresh basil
Salt and freshly ground black pepper
    to taste

Thirty-two 3-inch pasta squares
    (see page 111 or 117 for the dough,
    page 110 for cutting directions), or
    wonton wrappers

For the filling, combine the ricotta cheese, egg whites, sun-dried tomato, basil, salt, and black pepper in a bowl. Mix thoroughly.

Make the tortellini by mounding 2 teaspoons of the prepared filling in a corner of 1 pasta square and painting the border all around with water. Fold the corner diagonally opposite over the filling and press along the edges to seal. Fold each of the opposite tips of the triangle up to meet and crimp them together. Repeat the process until all the tortellini are filled.

To cook the tortellini, bring a pot of water to the boil. Add the tortellini and cook over medium heat until they rise to the top of the pot, about 3 minutes. Using a slotted spoon, remove them to a colander to drain. Serve 8 tortellini to each person.

Yield = 4 servings
Fat per serving = 0.68 g.
Calories per serving = 278.0

THESE DELICATE little morsels are filled with ricotta cheese, fresh basil, and sun-dried tomato, which flavors the pasta intensely since it is not reconstituted (that being the case, use sun-dried tomatoes that are reasonably pliable, not brittle). They're equally tasty made either with Homemade Pasta (page 111) or with Carrot Pasta (page 117). And believe it or not, they're pretty good made with wonton wrappers on those days when time is tight.

Our favorite way to serve these tortellini are to float them in Bean and Vegetable Stew (page 52). They also go well with Mushroom Sauce (page 127) and Yellow Pepper–Mushroom Sauce (page 132).

MORE ASSERTIVE IN flavor and hue than other noodles, spinach fettucine is nicely paired with Tomato-Mint Sauce (page 128) or Mushroom Sauce (page 127). We also use this pasta to make Roasted Tomato Ravioli (page 116).

Spinach Pasta

10 ounces fresh spinach, stemmed, washed, and dried

1½ cups all-purpose flour

4 to 5 tablespoons nonfat liquid egg substitute

Put the spinach into the bowl of a food processor and process to a coarse chop. Add the flour and process until well mixed. While pulsing, add the liquid egg substitute 1 tablespoon at a time, just until bits of dough the size of large peas form.

Turn the dough out onto a floured work surface and knead for about a minute until glossy and elastic. Form it into a ball, cover with plastic wrap, and set aside for 30 minutes.

Roll out and cut the dough into fettucine noodles according to the directions on page 109.

Yield = 6 servings, or enough dough for 32 pasta circles or squares
Fat per serving = 0.37 g.
Calories per serving = 109.3

Spinach Fettucine with Baccalà and Tomato

4 ounces dried salt cod

1 recipe Spinach Pasta (see page 114 for the dough, page 109 for cutting directions)

1 tablespoon salt

6 ounces cherry tomatoes (about 9 tomatoes), quartered

8 cloves roasted garlic, roughly chopped

Put the cod into a mixing bowl. Cover it with cold water, refrigerate, and let reconstitute for at least 12 hours. Rinse the cod in a colander under cold running water, drain, and transfer it to a medium saucepan. Add sufficient cold water to cover the fish by 1 inch. Bring to a boil over medium-high heat. Reduce the heat to low and simmer, uncovered, until the fish flakes easily, about 20 minutes. Drain, remove any residual skin or bone from the cod, and break the fish into large flakes.

Meanwhile, bring a large pot of water to a boil. Add the salt and the pasta. Cook until the pasta is *al dente*, 3 to 4 minutes. Drain and transfer the pasta to a serving bowl, reserving ¼ cup of the cooking liquid. Add the tomatoes, garlic, and flaked cod to the bowl, along with the reserved liquid. Toss to mix.

Yield = 6 servings
Fat per serving = 0.96 g.
Calories per serving = 179.2

OUR TERRACE OVER Lake Michigan feels like a slice of the Amalfi coast whenever we serve this simple yet evocative dish. Baccalà is cod that is salted when caught and then set out in the sun to dry. A staple of Mediterranean kitchens, it can be found in a variety of ethnic groceries, including African and Mexican as well as Italian, Greek, and Middle Eastern.

THIS RECIPE TAKES
some time for the slow
roasting of the tomatoes,
but not a lot of hands-on
effort. It works well with
Homemade Pasta (page 111)
and is particularly good
made with Spinach Pasta
(page 114). You can float the
ravioli in Garlic Broth (page
57) or in Bean and Vegetable
Stew (page 52), or sauce it
with Spicy Roasted Garlic
and Eggplant Sauce (page
125).

Roasted Tomato Ravioli

8 small plum tomatoes (about 2
 pounds), halved
1 teaspoon coarse salt
½ teaspoon freshly ground black
 pepper
1 cup water
1 cup skim-milk ricotta cheese
2 tablespoons chopped fresh flat-leaf
 parsley

Thirty-two 3-inch pasta squares (see
 page 111 or 114 for the dough, page
 110 for cutting directions), or
 wonton wrappers
16 leaves fresh basil
½ cup nonfat liquid egg substitute

Preheat the oven to 400 degrees.

Sprinkle the cut sides of the tomatoes with the coarse salt and the pepper
and place them cut side down in a baking dish. Add ½ cup of the water and
roast for 30 minutes.

Remove the pan and turn the oven down to 200 degrees. Remove the
tomatoes from the pan, pour off the pan juices, pull the skins off the tomatoes, and return them to the pan. Roast for about 2 hours more, until the
tomatoes are just beginning to look dry and leathery. Remove from the oven
and raise the temperature to 450 degrees.

In a small bowl, mix together the ricotta cheese and parsley.

In the center of each of 16 of the pasta squares, mound a tomato half, a
basil leaf, and 2 tablespoons of the ricotta mixture. Paint the outer borders
with the egg substitute. Place a second square on top of each and crimp the
edges to seal. Place the ravioli in the roasting pan and add the remaining ½
cup water. Cover with aluminum foil and return to the oven for 7 minutes
more, until cooked through.

Serve 4 ravioli to each person.

Yield = 4 servings
Fat per serving = 0.96 g.
Calories per serving = 298.5

Carrot Pasta

1¾ cups all-purpose flour   1 teaspoon salt
¾ cup semolina flour   1 cup carrot juice

Combine the flours and the salt in the bowl of a food processor. Process for about 1 minute to mix well. With the machine running, very slowly drizzle in the carrot juice through the feed tube until a ball forms. (You may not need to use the whole cup.) Continue to process for 1 minute more.

Remove the dough to a lightly floured work surface and knead it 10 to 12 times, until smooth and elastic.

Roll out and cut the dough into fettucine according to the directions on page 109, taking care to separate the strands.

Yield = 6 servings
Fat per serving = 0.94 g.
Calories per serving = 270.1

VIBRANTLY COLORED and subtly flavored carrot pasta is a good alternative to plain pasta for Ricotta and Basil Tortellini (page 113). The pasta goes well with seafood as well as with cheese; we encourage you to experiment with your own filling mixtures. Fashioned into fettucine, it is set off nicely by Yellow Pepper–Mushroom Sauce (page 132). In this recipe we use a little semolina, which is more characteristic of dried noodles, to provide extra body for the delicate pasta.

Look for organic carrot juice in your supermarket's freezer case.

Homemade Gnocchi

ALTHOUGH YOU CAN FIND decent ready-made gnocchi vacuum-packed in the supermarket these days, we think our own are better. Besides, they're easy to make and freeze well for up to a month; just toss them in a little potato flour and seal them in heavy-duty storage bags.

Homemade gnocchi are best accompanied by Tomato-Mint Sauce (page 128), Spicy Roasted Garlic and Eggplant Sauce (page 125), or Almost Leslie's Garlic-Parsley Sauce (page 133).

1 pound Yukon Gold potatoes (about 3 potatoes)
5 cups cold water

1 large egg white
¾ cup all-purpose flour

Combine the potatoes and water in a medium saucepan over medium heat. Cook, uncovered, for 30 minutes. Drain. While the potatoes are still hot, rub their skins off with a clean dish towel, taking care not to burn your hands.

Rice the peeled potatoes into a mixing bowl and let them cool for 2 to 3 minutes. Add the egg white and flour. With lightly floured hands, mix just until a soft dough holds together.

Break off small sections of dough and roll them out into 1-inch-thick ropes. Cut the ropes on the diagonal into ½-inch dumplings. Make a partial incision in the middle of each with the point of a sharp knife.

To cook the gnocchi, bring a large pot of water to a boil over high heat. Add the gnocchi to the boiling water and cook for about 3 minutes, until they rise to the top. Drain.

Yield = 4 servings
Fat per serving = 0.26 g.
Calories per serving = 144.6

Pumpkin Gnocchi

1 pound canned pure pumpkin puree
1 large egg white
¾ cup all-purpose flour

¾ teaspoon salt
1 teaspoon ground coriander
1 tablespoon potato flour

Combine the pumpkin, egg white, all-purpose flour, salt, and coriander in a mixing bowl. With lightly floured hands, mix just enough to form a cohesive, soft dough.

Using 1 rounded tablespoon of the dough for each, form about 4 dozen egg-shaped dumplings. Toss to coat in the potato flour. Make a partial incision in the middle of each with the point of a sharp knife.

To cook the gnocchi, bring a large pot of water to a boil over high heat. Add the gnocchi to the boiling water and cook for 6 to 8 minutes, until they rise to the top. Drain.

Yield = 4 servings
Fat per serving = 0.71 g.
Calories per serving = 131.2

If you like gnocchi, you'll love this intriguing variation, rich in pumpkin, which is popular in Lombardy, and spiked with just enough ground coriander to liven things up a bit. These gnocchi are smashing with Tomato-Oregano Sauce (page 131).

Sauces

(Salse)

Green Sauce — Spicy Roasted Garlic and Eggplant Sauce — Meat Sauce — Mushroom Sauce — Tomato-Mint Sauce — Grapefruit Sauce — Raw Tomato Sauce — Tomato-Oregano Sauce — Yellow Pepper–Mushroom Sauce — Almost Leslie's Garlic-Parsley Sauce

8. Sauces

(Salse)

Given the Italian devotion to pasta, saucing is a fundamental part of the cuisine. Sauces for our dried pasta dishes, which tend to be abundantly laced with vegetables and seafood, are part of each recipe. This chapter features sauces that pair well with the more delicate fresh pastas.

Once one overcomes the Italian propensity to start every sauce with a sizable dash of olive oil—we rely on wine and chicken stock instead—there are few pitfalls for the fat-free cook. These are simple tomato, vegetable, and herb preparations with little inherent fat.

Remember to sauce the pasta immediately after it is cooked and while both pasta and sauce are still warm. And take care to use a light touch; the sauce should accent the pasta, not drown it.

Many of these sauces work nicely with seafood as well. The Green Sauce is especially good on shrimp, the Tomato-Oregano Sauce suits salmon almost as well as it does pumpkin-flavored gnocchi, and the Yellow Pepper–Mushroom Sauce is every bit as good on tuna, swordfish, or shark steaks as on carrot pasta. Several of these sauces can be used to perk up a plain baked or broiled white fish fillet; indeed, this is the primary purpose of our Grapefruit Sauce.

Green Sauce

Our version of *salse verde* from Emilia-Romagna uses a little white wine and balsamic vinegar in lieu of the usual olive oil. We typically serve it on shrimp and rice or on medallions of monkfish that have been cooked in the sauce. A robust, somewhat assertive sauce, it is also good on either fresh or dried pasta, grilled scallops or salmon, and braised veal. For a unique treat, stir it into risotto just as you take the rice off the heat.

¾ cup fresh flat-leaf parsley leaves (about ½ bunch)
1 tablespoon capers, drained

1 small clove garlic, peeled
1 tablespoon balsamic vinegar
3 tablespoons dry white wine

Combine all ingredients in the bowl of a blender or food processor and puree to create a smooth sauce.

Yield = ¼ cup, or enough for 4 servings
Fat per serving = 0.04 g.
Calories per serving = 14.4

Spicy Roasted Garlic and Eggplant Sauce

1 pound purple eggplant (about 1
   small eggplant)

2 teaspoons coarse salt

Olive oil cooking spray

8 ounces yellow onion (about 1
   onion), chopped (about 1⅓ cups)

¼ cup dry white wine

12 cloves roasted garlic, chopped
   (about 2 tablespoons; see Pantry)

3 cups cut-up canned or boxed
   tomatoes with their juice

¼ teaspoon crushed red pepper flakes

We created this sauce to top Soft Polenta (page 174) and have since enjoyed it on fresh pastas of all sorts, on Homemade Gnocchi (page 118), and on broiled or grilled Herb Polenta (page 172). We've even spooned it onto crusty slices of Rustic Italian Bread (page 63) as a meal in itself. Make as much as you want—the sauce freezes and microwaves well.

Trim the eggplant and cut it into ½-inch cubes. Place the cubes in a colander and sprinkle with the coarse salt. Toss and allow to drain in the sink for 30 minutes. Rinse under cold water for about 1 minute, then wrap the cubes in paper towels and squeeze dry.

Meanwhile, preheat the oven to 350 degrees. Spray a baking sheet to coat with the olive oil spray.

Place the eggplant on the prepared sheet and bake for 15 minutes. Toss and bake for about 15 minutes more, until just beginning to brown.

Preheat a medium nonstick skillet over high heat. Add the onion and cook, stirring, until browned, 2 to 3 minutes. Add the wine and cook for about 1 minute more, until it has evaporated. Add the eggplant, roasted garlic, tomatoes, and crushed pepper. Reduce the heat to medium-low and cook for about 5 minutes, until very thick.

Yield = 4 cups, or enough for 4 servings
Fat per serving = 0.26 g.
Calories per serving = 127.2

We use fast-cooking turkey in this healthful version of a bolognese, so it doesn't have to simmer for hours. The sauce goes well with any fresh fettucine; simply toss with a little Parmesan cheese and chopped parsley. It also complements shaped dried pasta, lasagne, and several polentas—Soft Polenta (page 174), Sun-Dried Tomato Polenta (page 179), and Herb Polenta (page 172).

Meat Sauce

6 ounces carrots (about 2 carrots), finely chopped (about 1 cup)

6 ounces celery (about 2 stalks), finely chopped (about 1 cup)

6 ounces yellow onion (about 1 onion), chopped (about 1 cup)

2 cloves garlic, chopped

½ cup dry white wine

1 pound turkey breast tenderloin slices, ground (see Pantry)

1½ cups Chicken Stock (see page 19)

Salt to taste

In a medium nonstick skillet, combine the carrots, celery, onion, garlic, and ¼ cup of the wine. Cook over medium heat for 10 to 12 minutes, stirring periodically, until the onion turns translucent. Mix in the turkey. Stirring occasionally, cook for about 5 minutes, until the meat is no longer pink and has separated some. Add the stock and the remaining ¼ cup wine. Stir, raise the heat to high, and bring to a boil. Reduce the heat to medium-low, cover, and simmer for 45 minutes. Set the cover ajar and continue to cook for about 15 minutes more, until the liquid has mostly evaporated. Salt to taste.

Yield = 4 cups, or enough for 6 servings
Fat per serving = 0.91 g.
Calories per serving = 120.6

Mushroom Sauce

8 ounces cremini mushrooms, cleaned
and trimmed

1 clove garlic, peeled and cut into
chunks

2 ounces yellow onion, peeled and cut
into chunks (about ⅓ cup)

¾ cup dry white wine

2 teaspoons chopped fresh flat-leaf
parsley

Combine the mushrooms, garlic, and onion in a food processor and process to a fine chop. Transfer to a medium nonstick skillet. Cook over medium heat for 10 to 12 minutes, until the water given off by the mushrooms has been absorbed. Add the wine and cook for about 10 minutes more, until thick. Stir in the parsley.

Yield = ¾ cup, or enough for 6 servings
Fat per serving = 0.12 g.
Calories per serving = 34.5

THIS VEGETARIAN sauce is so hearty it could replace almost any meat ragù. We like it with Homemade Gnocchi (page 118), Stiff Polenta (page 175), Herb Polenta (page 172), and fettucine made with either Carrot Pasta (page 117) or Spinach Pasta (page 114). It's also quite good on such sturdy shaped pasta as rigatoni or penne, in a vegetable lasagne, or on sole or halibut.

READILY AVAILABLE
turmeric replaces pricey
saffron in this classic
tomato-and-mint pairing.
Serve it on grilled or broiled
fish or chicken, on fettucine
made from Spinach Pasta
(page 114), or on
Homemade Gnocchi
(page 118) or Herb Polenta
(page 172).

Tomato-Mint Sauce

6 large cloves garlic, minced

1 tablespoon chopped fresh mint
  leaves

1 cup dry white wine

1/8 teaspoon ground turmeric

1 cup cut-up, drained, canned or
  boxed tomatoes, or 12 ounces
  tomatoes (about 2 tomatoes), peeled,
  seeded, and chopped (about 1 cup)

Salt to taste

1/8 teaspoon crushed red pepper flakes

Preheat a medium skillet over medium heat. Add the garlic and cook for just a few seconds, stirring constantly, until it begins to give off an aroma. Add the mint leaves and stir twice to mix. Add the wine and turmeric and cook for about 2 minutes, until you can no longer smell the alcohol. Add the tomatoes, salt, and red pepper. Raise the heat to high and bring just to a boil. Reduce the heat to medium and cook for 20 to 22 minutes, stirring occasionally, until a thick sauce forms.

Yield = 1 cup, or enough for 4 servings
Fat per serving = 0.03 g.
Calories per serving = 74.4

Grapefruit Sauce

One 12-ounce ruby-red grapefruit

½ cup chopped white onion

2 tablespoons water

2 tablespoons all-purpose flour

½ cup dry white wine

2 tablespoons chopped fresh flat-leaf parsley

Salt and freshly ground black pepper to taste

THIS PUNGENT SAUCE will perk up any fillet of plain white fish, such as flounder, sole, or haddock. It's also superb on cod fillets baked at 450 degrees for about 12 minutes, until white and opaque.

Remove the zest from the grapefruit in large sections, taking care to avoid the pith. Immerse the zest in boiling water and boil for 5 minutes. Drain and hold in a strainer under cold running water until totally cooled, then pat dry with paper towels. Cut into thin strips. Juice the grapefruit (about ¾ cup). Set the juice aside.

Combine the onion and water over medium heat in a small saucepan. Cook for about 3 minutes, stirring occasionally, until the onion is limp and translucent. Meanwhile, combine the flour and wine in a small bowl and mix thoroughly. When the onion has cooked, add the grapefruit juice, then the flour-and-wine mixture. Stir to combine. Continue to cook over medium heat for another 8 to 10 minutes, stirring periodically, until the sauce is blended, thick, and creamy. Add the parsley, salt, and pepper and stir in 2 tablespoons of the grapefruit zest, using any leftover zest for garnish if desired.

Yield = 1 cup, or enough for 6 servings
Fat per serving = 0.07 g.
Calories per serving = 39.3

Raw Tomato Sauce

No prepping (no need to worry about seeding or peeling cherry tomatoes), no cooking, no chilling— just mix and serve this forthright sauce at room temperature, substituting an equal measure of chopped fresh basil for the parsley when you feel like a change. It is wonderful tossed on delicate fresh fettucine or drizzled on baked cod. Served with fish and a side dish of pasta, the sauce works equally well on both.

8 ounces cherry tomatoes (about 12 tomatoes)
2 cloves garlic, chopped

¼ cup chopped fresh flat-leaf parsley
3 tablespoons freshly squeezed lemon juice

Cut each tomato in half, then quarter each of the halves.

Combine all the ingredients in a bowl, mix thoroughly, and set aside for 15 minutes for the flavors to meld.

Yield = 1 cup, or enough for 4 servings
Fat per serving = 0.17 g.
Calories per serving = 15.8

Tomato-Oregano Sauce

2 scallions, trimmed to white and light
  green parts, minced (about 3
  tablespoons)
1 clove garlic, minced
½ tablespoon chopped fresh oregano
  (or ½ teaspoon dried)

⅛ teaspoon crushed red pepper flakes
¼ cup balsamic vinegar
1 medium tomato, peeled, seeded, and
  very finely diced (about ¾ cup)

In a small bowl, combine the scallions, garlic, oregano, crushed pepper, and vinegar. Mix and let sit for 10 minutes. Stir in the tomato.

Yield = 1 cup, or enough for 4 servings
Fat per serving = 0.13 g.
Calories per serving = 10.8

THIS VERSATILE uncooked sauce is the perfect accompaniment to salmon, either hot off the grill or poached and served cold. It's also quite good with roasted halibut or sea bass. We often serve it atop Pumpkin Gnocchi (page 119) or Stiff Polenta (page 175) as well.

Yellow Pepper-Mushroom Sauce

TRY THIS ROBUST, garlic-laden sauce with fettucine made from Carrot Pasta (page 117); leave the pasta slightly damp and toss it with a little Parmesan so that both the sauce and the cheese cling to the strands. It is also delicious with broiled or grilled slices of Sun-Dried Tomato Polenta (page 179). If you are pairing it with fish, choose meaty grilled steaks such as tuna, swordfish, or shark.

6 ounces cremini mushrooms, cleaned, trimmed, and very finely chopped
4 cloves garlic, peeled
2 tablespoons chopped fresh flat-leaf parsley

Salt and freshly ground black pepper to taste
4 ounces roasted yellow bell pepper (see Pantry), finely chopped (about ½ cup)
½ cup dry white wine

Preheat a medium nonstick skillet over medium heat. Add the mushrooms and cook for about 2 minutes, stirring, until they have given off their liquid. Press in the garlic. Stir in the parsley, salt, and black pepper. Cook 1 minute more. Stir in the roasted pepper, then the wine. Simmer for 10 to 12 minutes, until thick and rich.

Yield = ⅔ cup, or enough for 4 servings
Fat per serving = 0.22 g.
Calories per serving = 44.1

Almost Leslie's Garlic-Parsley Sauce

½ cup packed fresh flat-leaf parsley
   leaves
2 cloves garlic, smashed and peeled

½ cup bread crumbs (see Pantry)
2 tablespoons balsamic vinegar
1 cup Chicken Stock (see page 19)

Combine the parsley and garlic in a food processor. Process to a fine chop. Add the bread crumbs and vinegar. With the machine running, drizzle the stock through the feed tube to form a sauce.

Yield = ¾ cup, or enough for 6 servings
Fat per serving = 0.11 g.
Calories per serving = 19.8

THIS IS OUR FAT-FREE version of a garlic-parsley sauce featured in *Great Fish, Quick* by our buddy Leslie Revsin. The pretty pale green sauce, somewhat evocative of sauce *genovese*, stays fresh and flavorful for up to 3 days in the refrigerator. We replace red wine vinegar with balsamic vinegar to maintain the smoothness lent by oil in the original version. The sauce is good hot or at room temperature. Leslie recommends serving it on delicate white fish or as a dipping sauce for shrimp. We also like it with fresh pasta (pages 111 to 117) and with Homemade Gnocchi (page 118).

Fish and Shellfish

(Pesce e Frutti di Mare)

Monkfish Osso Buco ⌒ Mussels with Saffron Risotto ⌒
Baby Octopus Ragù ⌒ Roasted Cod with Fennel on Arugula
⌒ Sautéed Prawns ⌒ Baked Fish Fillets in Tomato-Leek
Sauce ⌒ Crispy Gnocchi with Clams and Mushrooms ⌒
Tilapia Bundles with Tomato-Caper Sauce ⌒ Cod Gratin
⌒ Fish in Acqua Pazza

9. Fish and Shellfish

(Pesce e Frutti di Mare)

Any question that may exist about the number of seafood dishes in Italian cuisine is quickly put to rest by a passing glance at a map. The mainland of Italy is surrounded by water on three sides, and then there are the islands. Only four regions in the far north and landlocked Umbria lack a coastline.

The wealth of local fish and shellfish has produced a profusion of preparations that can be replicated in the American kitchen. Of course, there are regional differences in the availability of seafood even within Italy, and many of the fish that live in Italian waters are all but impossible to find in the United States. Sea bass, tuna, monkfish, and swordfish, however, are available, as are crustaceans and mollusks. We also suggest using red snapper, cod, sole, flounder, and haddock, which adapt well to Italian recipes.

Seafood is a boon to fat-free cooking. The spectrum of flavors and textures is so broad and pleasing that people would eat it even if fat were of no concern. It is comforting to know, however, that a piece of cod or haddock has half the fat of an equal portion of skinless chicken breast, and that you could eat something in excess of 200 mussels instead of a modest serving of lean sirloin.

Our selection of seafood offerings ranges from simple roasted cod and sautéed prawns to a somewhat more exotic baby octopus ragù; monkfish fillets which we prepare in an osso buco fashion; a whole red snapper simmered with bay scallops in "crazy water"; and a magnificent dish of mussels atop saffron-infused risotto speckled with fava beans and tomato.

Monkfish Osso Buco

Firm, mild-tasting, and low-fat monkfish (sometimes called angler fish or goosefish) takes well to the Milanese preparation known as osso buco, usually reserved for veal shanks. The edible portion of the fish is its tail meat, which comes looking rather like a long thin tenderloin. Cut the fish into 4 pieces, creating medallions shaped like shanks.

Our sauce is made from traditional osso buco ingredients, except that we include the anchovy now typically added by American cooks and dispense with the *gremolata,* or sprinkle of garlic, lemon, and parsley, that Italians add after the veal has cooked. If you are timid about anchovies, have no fear; they are used in this recipe basically for richness and saltiness, and leave only the faintest hint of anchovy taste.

3 ounces carrot (about 1 carrot), diced (about ⅔ cup)

4 ounces yellow onion (about 1 small onion), diced (about ¾ cup)

3 small cloves garlic, minced

3 ounces celery (about 2 small stalks), diced (about ⅔ cup)

¾ cup Vegetable Stock (see page 20)

Two 3-by-1-inch strips orange peel

1 bay leaf

1 pound tomatoes (about 2 tomatoes), peeled, seeded, and chopped (about 1½ cups), or 1½ cups cut-up boxed or canned tomatoes with their juice

½ cup dry white wine

1 tablespoon chopped fresh basil

1 tablespoon chopped fresh flat-leaf parsley

½ teaspoon dried thyme

1 anchovy fillet, minced (see Pantry)

12 ounces monkfish, cut into 4 pieces

Salt and freshly ground black pepper to taste

1 tablespoon plus 1 teaspoon grated orange zest

Preheat a Dutch oven over high heat. Add the carrot, onion, garlic, and celery. Cook for about 2 minutes, until the vegetables have just started to color. Add ¼ cup of the stock, the orange peel, and the bay leaf. Cover and cook for about 4 minutes, until the vegetables are tender and dry. Add the tomatoes, wine, basil, parsley, thyme, anchovy, and the remaining ½ cup stock. Bring to a boil. Place the fish in the pot, cover, reduce the heat to medium-low, and cook for 10 minutes. Turn the fish over and cook for 10 minutes more.

Remove the fish, raise the heat to high, and boil for about 2 minutes to create a thick sauce. Add salt and pepper to taste. Remove the orange peel and bay leaf.

Top each serving of monkfish with ¾ cup of the sauce and garnish with 1 teaspoon of the grated orange zest.

Yield = 4 servings
Fat per serving = 0.96 g.
Calories per serving = 135.3

Mussels with Saffron Risotto

2 cups water
¼ teaspoon salt
1 pound fava beans, shelled
5 cups Chicken Stock (see page 19)
¼ teaspoon saffron
1½ cups Vialone Nano, Carnaroli, or
   Arborio rice

¼ cup dry white wine
1½ pounds debearded blue mussels
8 ounces tomato (about 1 tomato),
   peeled, seeded, and chopped (about
   1 cup)

Bring the water to a boil in a medium saucepan over high heat. Add the salt and the fava beans. Cook for 30 seconds, drain, and rinse under cold water. Peel the beans.

Bring the Chicken Stock to a boil in a medium saucepan. Add the saffron and reduce the heat to maintain a simmer.

Preheat a nonstick Dutch oven over high heat. Add the rice and cook, stirring constantly, until lightly browned, about 3 minutes. Keeping the heat on high, slowly add 1 cup of the stock, stirring vigorously. When the stock has been mostly absorbed and small craters dot the surface, add another ½ cup. Stir and bring back to a simmer. Add the remaining stock ½ cup at a time, stirring after each addition. Continue to stir until the liquid has been absorbed and the rice is creamy. Stir in the wine. Place the mussels over the rice. Cover, reduce the heat to medium, and cook until the mussels open, about 12 minutes, shaking the pan periodically. (Discard any mussels that do not open naturally while cooking.)

Remove the mussels to a bowl. Stir the fava beans and tomatoes into the risotto. Serve ¾ cup of rice per person, dividing the mussels equally and placing them on top.

Yield = 6 servings
Fat per serving = 0.77 g.
Calories per serving = 229.7

THIS SPECTACULAR dish, one of our favorites for entertaining, boasts lots of tender, juicy mussels. They sit on a bed of pale, creamy risotto that is infused with saffron in the Milanese fashion and speckled with succulent fava beans and ripe red tomatoes.

Take care to prevent the rice on the bottom of the pot from burning once you have added the mussels; make sure to reduce the heat to medium and shake the pot periodically. You can also cook the mussels separately while making the risotto. Steam them, covered, for 5 to 6 minutes in about ½ inch of white wine or water in a Dutch oven or large saucepan, until they open. Be sure to rinse the mussels first under cold running water, and discard any that don't close when tapped or that have broken shells.

THE BABY OCTOPUS that is the star of this spicy stew can be purchased trimmed and cleaned in Italian, Greek, and Asian markets. (You could also use cleaned small squid.) Whereas large octopus takes a bit of effort to prepare—Italians often first beat it to tenderize it, then boil it, sometimes along with a cork, which is supposed to add tenderizing enzymes to the water—tender baby octopus are more easily cooked; braise them slowly as you would squid, using low heat.

We like the ragù served with Soft Polenta (page 174), Stiff Polenta (page 175), Herb Polenta (page 172), or chunks of Rustic Italian Bread (page 63).

Baby Octopus Ragù

1 pound cleaned baby octopus
12 ounces tomatoes (about 2 small tomatoes), peeled, seeded, and chopped (about 1 cup), or 1 cup drained, cut-up boxed or canned tomatoes
3 cloves garlic, minced

3 tablespoons chopped fresh arugula
$\frac{1}{2}$ teaspoon salt
$\frac{1}{4}$ teaspoon freshly ground black pepper
4 drops hot sauce (optional)

Combine all the ingredients in a heavy medium saucepan. Cook over high heat for 1 to 2 minutes, stirring occasionally, just until the mixture begins to bubble. Cover, reduce the heat to the lowest possible setting, and cook for 40 to 50 minutes, until the octopus is fork-tender.

Remove the cover and continue to cook 15 to 20 minutes more, until the sauce has thickened.

Serve $\frac{1}{2}$ cup of stew to each person.

Yield = 6 servings
Fat per serving = 0.81 g.
Calories per serving = 77.9

Roasted Cod with Fennel on Arugula

Four 5-ounce cod fillets

¼ teaspoon dried thyme

Salt to taste

12 ounces fennel (about 1 bulb), cleaned, trimmed of the green stalks, quartered, and thinly sliced lengthwise (about 4 cups)

8 ounces yellow onion (about 1 onion), thinly sliced (about 2 cups)

⅔ cup dry white wine

12 ounces tomatoes (about 2 small tomatoes), cored, seeded, and chopped (about 1 cup)

Juice of 1 lemon

1 bunch arugula, trimmed (about 6 ounces leaves), cut into bite-sized pieces (about 6 cups)

Preheat the oven to 450 degrees.

Arrange the cod fillets in a single layer in a baking dish. Sprinkle them with the thyme and salt and bake for about 15 minutes, until cooked through and easily flaked. Remove from the oven.

Preheat a large nonstick skillet over medium heat. Add the fennel, onion, and wine. Cover and cook for about 10 minutes, until the fennel is fork-tender. Stir in the tomatoes and remove from the heat. Squeeze in the lemon juice.

Put 1½ cups of the arugula on each of 4 dinner plates. Top each with a cod fillet and 1 cup of the fennel mixture.

Yield = 4 servings
Fat per serving = 0.94 g.
Calories per serving = 202.9

THE ITALIAN CULINARY master Marcella Hazan advises cooks to choose the variety of fennel, or *finocchio,* that has a round stocky bulb rather than that with a long flat bulb. The former is left longer in the sun and so has a sweeter taste, whereas the elongated variety is bred to ripen quickly. We leave the core intact and slice the fennel very thin with a mandoline so that the tender leaves fan out from the core, which also provides a slightly chewy contrast. However, you can core the bulb after quartering it if you prefer a more uniform texture.

In this recipe we use a kind of large pink shrimp, now farm-raised in many parts of the United States, that our fishmonger calls freshwater prawns. They approximate Mediterranean prawns. More important, they afford those of us who live in such landlocked locales as the Midwest the rare pleasure of enjoying fresh shrimp.

We like to serve the prawns over fettucine made from Homemade Pasta (page 111) or from Spinach Pasta (page 114), over Soft Polenta (page 174), or alongside Tuscan Bread Salad (page 207).

Sautéed Prawns

1 pound freshwater prawns in their shells
1/2 cup freshly squeezed lemon juice
1/2 teaspoon salt
1/2 teaspoon freshly ground black pepper

1 large clove garlic, chopped
1/2 tablespoon dried rosemary, crumbled

Using scissors, make a cut along the outer, curved side of each prawn and hold it under running water to rinse out the black vein.

Combine the cleaned prawns with the lemon juice, salt, pepper, garlic, and rosemary in a glass or other nonreactive bowl. Cover and marinate for about 1 hour in the refrigerator, stirring periodically.

Preheat a large nonstick skillet over high heat. Transfer the contents of the bowl to the hot pan. Cook the prawns for about 2 minutes on each side, until the shells turn bright pink and the meat is opaque.

Remove to a serving bowl and set another alongside for the shells.

Yield = 4 servings
Fat per serving = 0.54 g.
Calories per serving = 90.6

Baked Fish Fillets in Tomato-Leek Sauce

Olive oil cooking spray

1 baby leek (about 2 ounces), cleaned, trimmed, halved lengthwise, and sliced (about ⅔ cup)

20 ounces haddock fillets

Salt and freshly ground black pepper to taste

¼ cup dry white wine

12 ounces tomatoes (about 2 tomatoes), peeled, seeded, and chopped (about 1 cup), or 1 cup drained, cut-up canned or boxed tomatoes

½ cup evaporated skim milk

IN THIS SIMPLE preparation, the leek first keeps the fish fillets from sticking to the dish as they bake and then lends just a hint of flavoring to the tomato sauce. Select a baking dish that will hold the fish fillets in a single layer with a slight overlap.

Preheat the oven to 350 degrees.

Spray a baking dish lightly with the olive oil and spread the oil to cover the bottom. Scatter the leek evenly in the dish. Bake for about 5 minutes, until the leek is tender but not yet colored. Remove the baking dish, leaving the oven on.

Season the fillets with salt and a generous amount of black pepper and lay them on top of the leek. Return the pan to the oven and bake for 10 minutes. Pour the wine over the fillets and bake about 4 minutes more, until they have turned opaque. Remove the fish to a platter and cover with aluminum foil to keep warm.

Strain the contents of the baking dish into a small saucepan, discarding the leek. Stir, and add the tomatoes and evaporated milk. Cook over medium-high heat for about 4 minutes, until the mixture is creamy and steaming but the tomatoes have not yet cooked down. Stir periodically, taking care not to let the mixture come to a boil.

Spoon about 6 tablespoons of the sauce over each serving of fish.

Yield = 4 servings
Fat per serving = 0.91 g.
Calories per serving = 151.8

Crispy Gnocchi with Clams and Mushrooms

WE THINK THIS preparation offers a nice alternative to plain boiled gnocchi. Here, already-cooked gnocchi are sautéed with clams and a mélange of mushrooms. Since wonderful fresh Italian porcini mushrooms are hard to find in the United States, one must make do with such substitutes as shiitakes, portobellos, or cremini, which are baby portobellos. Some cooks also like to use one of these varieties combined with dried porcinis.

1 prepared recipe Homemade Gnocchi (page 118), or 1 pound commercially prepared potato gnocchi
8 ounces cremini mushrooms, cleaned, trimmed, and cut into ½-inch cubes
8 ounces shiitake mushrooms, cleaned, trimmed, and cut into ½-inch cubes

2 large cloves garlic
½ tablespoon chopped fresh sage
1 tablespoon chopped fresh thyme
2 cups dry white wine
⅔ cup clam juice
1¼ pounds littleneck clams
2 tablespoons chopped fresh flat-leaf parsley
½ cup chopped arugula
Olive oil cooking spray

Bring a large pot of water to a boil over high heat. Add the gnocchi to the boiling water and cook for about 3 minutes, until the dumplings rise to the top of the pot. Drain and set aside.

Preheat a large nonstick skillet over medium-high heat. Add the mushrooms and cook for about 2 minutes, stirring constantly, until well browned. Press in the garlic. Add the sage and thyme. While stirring, cook for about 10 seconds more, until the garlic is just beginning to become aromatic. Add the wine, clam juice, and clams and cook 8 to 10 minutes, until the liquid is reduced by 75 percent and the clams open. Remove the clams to a bowl, discarding any that have not opened, and cover them with aluminum foil. Remove the pan from the heat and stir in the parsley and arugula.

While the clams cook, preheat a medium nonstick skillet over high heat.

In a bowl, spray the gnocchi twice lightly with olive oil and toss to coat. Add them to the heated pan. Cook for 4 to 5 minutes, tossing regularly, until well browned. Add the mushroom mixture and cook for 1 to 2 minutes over high heat to warm through.

Serve about 1¼ cups to each person, with the clams divided equally among the servings.

Yield = 4 servings
Fat per serving = 0.86 g.
Calories per serving = 313.4

Tilapia Bundles with Tomato-Caper Sauce

ITALIANS ARE FOND of thin slices of meat or fish layered with other ingredients or seasonings and rolled up, called *involtini*. A typical combination would be anchovies and cheese rolled in veal. Here we roll up a classically seasoned bread crumb mixture in tasty, low-fat tilapia, a fairly new, farm-raised variety of white fish. Freezing the rolls for a few minutes between assembling and cooking firms them up and helps keep their shape.

⅔ cup minced white onion

¾ cup dry white wine

4 large cloves garlic, peeled

¼ cup chopped fresh flat-leaf parsley

3 tablespoons bread crumbs (see Pantry)

2 teaspoons anchovy paste

¼ cup nonfat liquid egg substitute, or 2 large egg whites

Salt and freshly ground black pepper to taste

Six 3-ounce tilapia fillets

Olive oil cooking spray

12 ounces tomato (about 2 tomatoes), peeled, seeded, and chopped (about 1 cup), or 1 cup cut-up boxed or canned tomatoes with their juice

1 teaspoon small capers (nonpareils), drained

½ teaspoon Dried Seasoning Blend (see page 22)

Preheat a medium nonstick skillet over medium-high heat. Add the onion and ¼ cup of the wine. Press in 2 cloves of the garlic. Stirring constantly, cook until the onion is translucent and the wine has evaporated, 1 to 2 minutes. Remove from the heat and stir in the parsley, bread crumbs, and anchovy paste. Let cool for about 2 minutes, then transfer the mixture to a small bowl and stir in the egg substitute or egg whites, salt, and pepper.

Spread a generous 5 teaspoons of the mixture over each of the tilapia fillets. Roll up the fillets lengthwise around the filling and secure them closed with toothpicks. Arrange the rolls on a plate and put them in the freezer for 10 minutes to firm.

Again preheat a medium nonstick skillet over medium-high heat. Spray the tilapia rolls lightly with the olive oil, turning to coat them evenly. Place them in the hot skillet and cook for about 2 minutes, rotating them to brown evenly. Remove them to a platter.

Reduce the heat to medium. Press the remaining 2 cloves garlic into the skillet. Stir 2 to 3 times and add the remaining ½ cup wine. Cook for about 1 minute, until most of the wine has evaporated. Add the tomatoes, capers, and seasoning blend and cook for 1 minute more.

Return the fish to the pan and cook for 5 minutes. Turn and cook about 3 minutes more, until opaque and cooked through.

Yield = 6 servings
Fat per serving = 0.91 g.
Calories per serving = 105.0

THIS TRADITIONAL gratin boasts a novel seasoning twist—although rosemary is popular in Italian cuisine, it is usually used to flavor meats, or on occasion shellfish. We like it with white fish as well, and think you will too after trying this recipe. In fact, feel free to increase to up to 4 teaspoonsful the amount of rosemary you use in the chunky coulis with which the fish is ringed.

Cod Gratin

8 ounces white onion (about 1 large onion), chopped (about 1½ cups)
3 to 4 cloves garlic, minced
2 tablespoons plus ⅓ cup dry white wine
2 teaspoons dried rosemary, crushed
1¼ pounds tomatoes (about 3 tomatoes), peeled, seeded, and chopped (about 2 cups), or 2 cups drained, cut-up canned or boxed tomatoes

Four 6-ounce cod fillets
Salt and freshly ground black pepper to taste
1 cup bread crumbs (see Pantry)
¼ cup chopped fresh flat-leaf parsley

Preheat the oven to 375 degrees.

Combine the onion, garlic, and 2 tablespoons of the wine in a medium nonstick skillet over medium heat. Cook for 7 to 9 minutes, stirring frequently, until the onion is translucent. Add the rosemary and tomatoes. Stirring constantly, cook for about 20 seconds more, until the liquid has evaporated and the mixture looks dry. Remove from the heat.

Spread half of the mixture (about 1½ cups) over the bottom of a 13-by-9-by-2-inch baking dish. Lay the cod fillets on top and season with salt and pepper to taste. Top with the rest of the tomato mixture. Pour the remaining ⅓ cup wine over the mixture. Mix the bread crumbs and parsley and sprinkle over the dish. Bake for 25 to 30 minutes, until the fish is opaque in the center.

Yield = 4 servings
Fat per serving = 0.99 g.
Calories per serving = 233.0

𝒮PINACH FETTUCINE WITH BACCALÀ AND TOMATO

MUSSELS WITH SAFFRON RISOTTO

SHRIMP AND ZUCCHINI AGNOLOTTI

PARMESAN—RED PEPPER CUSTARD WITH TOMATO COULIS

PANETTONE BREAD
PUDDING
(*foreground*) AND
MILANESE PANETTONE

VEAL SPIEDINI AND SKEWERED LEMON TURKEY

RIGATONI WITH
ARTICHOKES, FAVA
BEANS, AND ARUGULA

BREAKFAST POLENTA

ROASTED PEPPER AND TOMATO TART IN A ROASTED POLENTA SHELL

Fish in Acqua Pazza

1 pound tomatoes (about 2 tomatoes), peeled, seeded, and chopped (about 1½ cups), or 1½ cups cut-up boxed or canned tomatoes with their juice

2 tablespoons chopped fresh flat-leaf parsley, plus additional for garnish

¼ teaspoon crushed red pepper flakes

½ teaspoon salt

2 large cloves garlic, minced

¾ cup dry white wine

1 cup water

One 1-pound whole red snapper, cleaned

1 pound bay scallops

In a large nonstick skillet, combine the tomatoes, parsley, crushed red pepper, salt, and garlic. Stir to combine. Stir in the wine and water. Bring to a boil over high heat and boil for 3 minutes.

Add the snapper. (There should be enough liquid in the pan to cover the fish halfway up; add a little more water if needed.) Reduce the heat to medium to maintain a simmer, cover, and cook for 7 minutes. Add the scallops, cover again, and cook for 3 to 4 minutes more, until the scallops are opaque and the tip of a knife easily pierces the thickest part of the snapper.

Remove the fish, reserving the cooking water. Fillet the snapper and place it on a long serving platter or directly onto dinner plates. Surround it with the scallops and drizzle with the *acqua pazza*. Garnish with chopped parsley.

Yield = 6 servings
Fat per serving = 0.53 g.
Calories per serving = 112.9

OUR INTRODUCTION TO fish in "crazy water" was at a Spanish-influenced restaurant that cooked fish in *agua loco,* but we've since become familiar with the Neapolitan dish whose spicy broth is known as *acqua pazza.* The poaching liquid contains a mix of tomatoes, garlic, parsley, and red pepper, to which wine is sometimes added. We dispense with the usual generous dollop of olive oil because of its fat content, and poach bay scallops along with the whole fish for added flavor.

Meat and Poultry

(Carne e Pollame)

Veal Spiedini ⌒ Skewered Lemon Turkey ⌒ Quail Ragù ⌒ Veal- and Couscous-Stuffed Red Peppers ⌒ Spaghetti and Meatballs ⌒ Turkey with Mushrooms, Zucchini, and Fennel ⌒ Turkey alla Cacciatora ⌒ Chicken Piccata ⌒ Stuffed Artichokes ⌒ Pork alla Romana

10. Meat and Poultry

(Carne e Pollame)

Somewhat surprisingly, this is perhaps the chapter in which the least adaptation is necessary to make Italian cooking fat-free. Italians have always used meat in much the same fashion as we do—as an accent, rather than as the center of attention in the typical American manner. Poverty, geography, and religion (Catholics will remember all those meatless days) combined to make meat an occasional commodity for so long that even now, in times of prosperity, easy food transport, and relaxed rituals, Italians still use meat sparingly.

At one time, cattle were worked to quite an age, and young beef was restricted to the diet of the old and infirm. As Carol Field notes in *In Nonna's Kitchen*, the saying was that "when veal and a person appear at table, one of them must be sick." Thus, Italians learned to prepare meat in harmony with other foods. They made stews, stuffed vegetables with meat, cut meat thin and rolled it around other ingredients, and, as in Asian cuisine, cut meat up and cooked it with vegetables.

We've employed many of these traditional methods in our attempt to make a little meat go a long way. We make turkey stews, braise pork with multicolored strips of bell pepper, stuff peppers with a veal mixture and artichokes with ground turkey, and use succulent quail in a ragù. Chicken breast pounded thin is the basis for a piccata preparation, and thin strips of turkey and veal are threaded onto skewers with vegetables for *spiedini*.

Veal Spiedini

Spiedini, THE ITALIAN version of brochettes, make a light yet filling meal. For a heartier meal, serve them with your favorite risotto. We particularly like to make *spiedini* in the summer, when the cooking can easily shift from the broiler to the outdoor grill. In this recipe, the veal first marinates in a flavorful Marsala wine mixture. You will need eight 8-inch skewers. If you use bamboo rather than metal skewers, be sure to soak them as directed to prevent charring. The addition of such baby vegetables as pattypan squash and teardrop or small cherry tomatoes in assorted colors lends a festive air.

Two 4-ounce veal scaloppine cutlets, each trimmed and cut into 4 long, thin strips
16 medium white button mushrooms (about 8 ounces), cleaned and halved
1/2 cup Marsala wine
1 teaspoon freshly ground black pepper
1/4 cup bread crumbs (see Pantry)
1 tablespoon finely chopped fresh flat-leaf parsley
1 teaspoon freshly grated Parmigiano-Reggiano cheese

If using bamboo skewers, soak them in water for at least 1 hour.

Put the strips of veal and the mushrooms into a shallow bowl. Add the wine and pepper and marinate at room temperature for 30 minutes, stirring every 5 minutes.

Preheat the broiler.

Mix together the bread crumbs, parsley, and Parmesan.

Thread a strip of veal onto each skewer in a serpentine fashion, interspersing 4 mushroom chunks between the folds of veal, ending with a mushroom on top. Roll in the bread crumb mixture to coat.

Position 4 inches from the heat source and broil for 3 minutes, until well browned. Turn and broil until well browned on the other side, about 4 minutes more.

Yield = 8 skewers
Fat per skewer = 0.68 g.
Calories per skewer = 53.4

Skewered Lemon Turkey

Four 3-ounce turkey breast tenderloin slices, each trimmed and cut in half lengthwise

¼ cup freshly squeezed lemon juice

¼ teaspoon freshly ground black pepper, plus additional to taste

Two 6-ounce zucchini

¼ cup plus 2 tablespoons bread crumbs (see Pantry)

2 tablespoons chopped fresh flat-leaf parsley

1 teaspoon grated lemon zest

Coarse salt to taste

16 purple pearl onions, peeled

Lemon wedges for garnish

You will need eight 8-inch skewers. If using bamboo rather than metal skewers, soak them in water for at least 1 hour.

Combine the turkey strips, lemon juice, and ¼ teaspoon of the black pepper in a shallow bowl and set aside at room temperature to marinate for 20 minutes.

Meanwhile, cut the zucchini crosswise into 6 pieces, then quarter each piece. Set aside. Mix together the bread crumbs, parsley, and lemon zest. Add salt and black pepper to taste.

Preheat the broiler.

Thread a strip of turkey onto each skewer in a serpentine fashion, interspersing the folds with 3 chunks of zucchini. Put a pearl onion at each end of each skewer. Roll the skewers in the bread crumb mixture to coat. Position 4 inches from the heat source and broil for about 4 minutes per side, until well browned.

Serve with lemon wedges on the side.

Yield = 8 skewers
Fat per skewer = 0.55 g.
Calories per skewer = 61.1

TURKEY IS POPULAR IN many regions of Italy, and on occasion is even elaborately stuffed or molded for holiday celebrations. For these considerably simpler and more informal brochettes, strips of turkey are marinated in a peppery lemon mixture, then coated in bread crumbs seasoned with parsley and lemon zest. Look for turkey breast tenderloin, the leanest cut available. We usually serve the skewers with Lemon Risotto (page 81), a heavenly pairing to those of us who love citrus.

Quail Ragù

THIS DISH IS VERY much in the Italian tradition of using meat as an accent rather than as the main component of a dish. Like many Italian stews and sauces, the ragù begins with a *soffritto*, an onion, celery, carrot, and garlic mixture that we cook in water instead of oil. The ragù derives its character from succulent little quails, which are showing up more and more frequently these days in supermarket freezers; they're also stocked by both Italian and Asian markets.

We usually serve a small amount of the intensely flavorful ragù atop slices of grilled or broiled Sun-Dried Tomato Polenta (page 179)—a rich and satisfying combination. It would also be good served over a hearty pasta, such as rigatoni.

¼ cup finely diced onion
¼ cup finely diced celery
¼ cup finely diced carrot
1 clove garlic, chopped
2 tablespoons water
6 ounces quail breast meat (3 to 4 quails), diced (about ¾ cup)
1 cup Chianti or other dry red wine
½ teaspoon chopped fresh rosemary
1 teaspoon chopped fresh sage
1 bay leaf
12 ounces tomatoes (about 2 small tomatoes), peeled, seeded, and chopped (about 1 cup), or 1 cup cut-up boxed or canned tomatoes with their juice
1 tablespoon sun-dried tomato paste

Preheat a nonstick Dutch oven over medium heat. Add the onion, celery, carrot, garlic, and water. Cook, stirring, until the water evaporates, 2 to 3 minutes. Add the quail and continue to cook and stir until the meat is no longer pink, about 2 minutes. Add the wine, raise the heat to high, and boil to reduce the volume by about half. Add the rosemary, sage, bay leaf, and tomatoes. Bring back to a boil, then reduce the heat to low. Cover and simmer for about 35 minutes, until the quail is tender.

Stir in the tomato paste and cook, uncovered, for about 10 minutes, until the mixture is thick but not dry. Serve a generous ¼ cup to each person.

Yield = 6 servings
Fat per serving = 0.94 g.
Calories per serving = 84.4

Veal- and Couscous-Stuffed Red Peppers

⅓ cup precooked couscous

½ cup boiling water

4 ounces portobello mushroom (about 1 mushroom), diced (about 1 cup)

⅔ cup diced yellow onion

1 large clove garlic, peeled

4 ounces veal scaloppine, trimmed and diced (about ½ cup)

¼ cup chopped fresh flat-leaf parsley

1 large egg white, beaten

Salt and freshly ground black pepper to taste

2 pounds tomatoes (about 4 tomatoes), peeled, seeded, and chopped (about 3 cups), or 3 cups cut-up boxed or canned tomatoes with their juice

2 teaspoons Dried Seasoning Blend (see page 22)

Four 6-ounce red bell peppers, halved lengthwise (including the stem), seeded and deveined

Combine the couscous and boiling water in a bowl. Cover and set aside.

Sauté the mushroom, onion, and garlic in a medium nonstick skillet over high heat until the onion begins to turn brown, 5 to 6 minutes. Add the veal and continue to cook and stir until the veal is no longer pink, about 45 seconds. Stir in the parsley, egg white, salt, black pepper, 1 cup of the tomatoes, and 1 teaspoon of the seasoning blend. Remove from the heat and stuff each half bell pepper with a generous ¼ cup of the mixture.

In a large skillet, combine the remaining 2 cups tomatoes and 1 teaspoon seasoning blend. Place the stuffed peppers in the skillet and bring to a boil over high heat. Reduce the heat to medium-low, cover, and cook for about 30 minutes, until the peppers are fork-tender.

Yield = 4 servings
Fat per serving = 0.93 g.
Calories per serving = 166.0

ALTHOUGH COUSCOUS is integral to Arab-Sicilian cuisine, it is also found in Sardinian dishes, lending credence to the speculation proposed by Mediterranean food maven Paula Wolfert that couscous arrived by way of Tunisia, which is equidistant from both islands.

In this recipe, we start with precooked couscous (sold in supermarkets near the rice), which can be prepared in a fraction of the time it would take to make the rice with which peppers are usually stuffed. We also replace the typical green pepper with the sweeter red variety. We prefer to use free-range veal, which is a bit darker in color and more emphatic in flavor than milk-fed veal.

Spaghetti and Meatballs

We just couldn't resist the temptation to include a version of the first "Italian" dish to which most Americans of a certain age were exposed. We don't know if anyone is certain of the derivation of this combination, although Michele Scicolone reports one theory in *A Fresh Taste of Italy*—that it was invented early in the century by American dietitians who were trying to introduce more protein into the typical pasta diet of Italian immigrants.

By starting with turkey breast tenderloin rather than preground turkey, which may contain hidden fat, you keep fat content to a minimum. We chop it along with the seasonings in the food processor. The meatballs are then baked, not pan-fried in oil. Peppery arugula is a major flavor component in both the meatballs and the versatile sauce, which would work nicely in almost any recipe that calls for a tomato-based sauce.

4 sun-dried tomatoes
1/4 cup hot water
Olive oil cooking spray
6 ounces turkey breast tenderloin slices, cut into chunks
1/2 cup bread crumbs (see Pantry)
1/4 cup nonfat liquid egg substitute, or 2 large egg whites
1/4 cup chopped white onion
1 clove garlic, minced
1/4 cup chopped arugula
Salt and freshly ground black pepper to taste
1/8 teaspoon crushed red pepper flakes
2 tablespoons skim milk

SAUCE:
1/4 cup diced white onion
2 tablespoons reserved sun-dried tomato soaking liquid
3 large cloves garlic, minced
1/4 cup chopped arugula
1 1/2 cups cut-up boxed or canned tomatoes with their juice, or 1 pound tomatoes (about 2 tomatoes), peeled, seeded, and chopped (about 1 1/2 cups)
1/8 teaspoon crushed red pepper flakes
6 ounces dried spaghetti

For the meatballs, combine the sun-dried tomatoes and water in a small bowl and set aside for 30 minutes for the tomatoes to reconstitute. Drain the tomatoes, reserving the soaking liquid, and chop (about 2 tablespoons).

Preheat the oven to 425 degrees. Spray a baking sheet with the olive oil.

Combine the reconstituted tomatoes with the turkey, bread crumbs, egg substitute or egg whites, onion, garlic, arugula, salt, black pepper, red pepper, skim milk, and 2 tablespoons of the tomato soaking liquid in the bowl of a food processor. Process until the mixture is finely ground and has formed a large ball.

Using about 1 1/2 tablespoons for each, form 12 meatballs. Place them on the prepared sheet and bake for about 9 minutes, until crisp and brown, shaking the pan every 3 minutes. Remove from the oven and set aside.

For the sauce, preheat a medium skillet over medium-high heat. Add the onion and the remaining 2 tablespoons of the tomato soaking liquid and cook for about 2 minutes, until the onion is translucent and the mixture is almost dry. Stir in the garlic and arugula. Add the tomatoes and red pepper. Reduce the heat to medium and cook for 10 minutes. Add the meatballs and cook for about 5 minutes more, until the sauce is thick and dry. Remove the meatballs with a slotted spoon.

Meanwhile, bring a large pot of water to a boil. Salt the water, add the spaghetti, and cook until the pasta is *al dente*. Drain and toss with the sauce. For each portion, serve 1 cup pasta and 3 meatballs.

Yield = 4 servings
Fat per serving = 1.00 g.
Calories per serving = 270.8

Turkey with Mushrooms, Zucchini, and Fennel

Stews are prevalent in Italian cooking, probably for the same reason we like them in fat-free cooking— a little meat goes a long way. This is a substantial stew, brimming with mushrooms, zucchini, and fennel as well as turkey. It goes nicely with Soft Polenta (page 174) or with plain white rice.

Because the recipe calls for whisking a flour mixture into a saucepan of hot stock, use a nonstick pan lined with the new scratch-resistant coating or an uncoated pan; otherwise, you could be left with a scarred surface.

3 cups Chicken Stock (see page 19)
½ cup freshly squeezed lemon juice
10 ounces turkey breast tenderloin
12 ounces fennel (about 1 bulb), trimmed and cut lengthwise into 8 wedges
4 ounces *cipolline* (small white onions), peeled and quartered
2 cloves garlic, peeled
8 ounces zucchini (about 2 small zucchini), trimmed and quartered crosswise, then quartered lengthwise

4 ounces white button mushrooms (about 8 mushrooms), cleaned, trimmed, and quartered
2 tablespoons all-purpose flour
½ cup nonfat liquid egg substitute
2 tablespoons chopped fresh dill
Salt and freshly ground black pepper to taste

In a medium saucepan, bring the Chicken Stock and lemon juice to a boil over high heat. Add the turkey, fennel, and *cipolline*. Press in the garlic. Reduce the heat to medium-low and simmer for 7 minutes.

Add the zucchini and mushrooms. Cover again and cook for about 8 minutes more, until the turkey is firm and the vegetables fork-tender. With a slotted spoon, remove the meat to a cutting board and the vegetables to a bowl. Remove and set aside ¼ cup of the stock. Cut the turkey into 1-inch cubes (about 1½ cups).

Bring the remaining stock back to a boil over high heat and boil until reduced to a volume of 2 cups, about 5 minutes. Remove from the heat.

Meanwhile, combine the reserved ¼ cup stock and the flour in a small bowl. Whisk until smooth. Whisk in the egg substitute until smoothly blended. While whisking the stock, add the mixture all at once. Return to low heat and cook for 2 minutes, whisking constantly, until the sauce has thickened. Stir in the turkey, vegetables, and dill. Salt and pepper to taste. Cook for 2 to 3 minutes more until heated through. Serve a generous 1 cup of the stew to each person.

Yield = 6 servings
Fat per serving = 0.90 g.
Calories per serving = 105.1

most commonly associated
with this homey dish, but
the recipe is said to have
first been made by hunters
with venison. Our rendition
uses turkey, whose low fat
content allows for generous
portions. Meaty portobello
mushrooms make the dish
even heartier and are
evocative of the wild
mushrooms the hunters
would have included in the
original version.

The cacciatora pairs well
with broiled or grilled slices
of Stiff Polenta (page 175).

Turkey alla Cacciatora

8 ounces yellow onion (about 1
 onion), peeled and sliced
10 ounces green bell pepper (about 1
 large pepper), cored, seeded, and
 thinly sliced
2 tablespoons water
2 ounces portobello mushroom (about
 1 cap), thinly sliced
2 cloves garlic, chopped
8 ounces turkey breast tenderloin slices,
 trimmed and cut into thin strips
3 cups cut-up boxed or canned
 tomatoes with their juice, or 2
 pounds tomatoes (about 4
 tomatoes), peeled, seeded, and
 chopped (about 3 cups)

1 bay leaf
1/2 tablespoon dried oregano
1 teaspoon dried basil
1/4 teaspoon celery seed
1/2 teaspoon freshly ground black
 pepper
Salt to taste
2 tablespoons small capers
 (nonpareils), drained

Preheat a large skillet over medium-high heat. Add the onion, bell pepper, and water. Sauté until the onion has turned translucent, about 3 minutes. Add the mushroom and garlic. Sauté for 1 minute more. Add the turkey and continue to sauté for another 1 to 2 minutes, until the meat is no longer pink. Add the tomatoes, bay leaf, oregano, basil, celery seed, black pepper, and salt. Bring to a boil. Cover, reduce the heat to medium-low, and cook for 20 minutes.

Stir the capers into the mixture in the skillet. Serve about 1 1/4 cups to each person.

Yield = 4 servings
Fat per serving = 0.98 g.
Calories per serving = 156.4

Chicken Piccata

¼ cup all-purpose flour

Four 3-ounce chicken cutlets

3½ ounces shiitake mushrooms, cleaned, stemmed, and sliced (about 1½ cups)

Olive oil cooking spray

Salt to taste

½ cup dry white wine

2 tablespoons freshly squeezed lemon juice

1 tablespoon chopped fresh flat-leaf parsley

Put the flour onto a plate. Pat the chicken in the flour to coat very lightly all over.

Preheat a large nonstick skillet over medium heat. Add the mushrooms and cook until they begin to soften, 2 to 3 minutes. Push the mushrooms to one side of the pan with a wooden spoon. Spray each cutlet lightly on both sides with the olive oil and place them in the pan in a single layer. Cook until the edges are cooked and firm, 1 to 2 minutes. Turn the cutlets and allow them to cook through, about 2 minutes longer. Lightly salt the chicken, add the wine, and continue to cook until you can no longer smell the wine, about 2 minutes more. Stir in the lemon juice and remove from the heat.

Sprinkle the parsley over individual servings as a garnish.

Yield = 4 servings
Fat per serving = 0.74 g.
Calories per serving = 174.1

ALTHOUGH VEAL IS more commonly used for this preparation, we rather like chicken lightly sautéed and dressed with lemon and parsley. Use chicken cutlets, which are breasts pounded as thin as veal scaloppine. Most butchers will do this for you. To prepare cutlets at home, slice a boneless split breast in half horizontally. Place each piece between sheets of wax paper and pound thin with a rolling pin or mallet.

After patting the chicken with flour, brush off any excess; the lighter the coating, the better the cutlet will brown without oil.

Stuffed Artichokes

ARTICHOKES, COOKED in almost any way imaginable, are tremendously popular throughout all regions of Italy. According to restaurateur and author Joyce Goldstein, artichokes, like eggplant and fennel, are among the foods introduced to Italy by Jewish settlers that have since become staples in all Italian kitchens.

Here's our rendition of a Tuscan-style stuffed artichoke. To trim the artichoke, cut the stem flush with the base and then clip the sharp point at the tip of each leaf with scissors. Unlike Italian artichokes or baby artichokes, which have softer chokes, the full-size American variety has chokes that are tough and must be removed; a grapefruit spoon does the trick nicely.

Two 12-ounce artichokes, trimmed (see sidebar)
2 tablespoons fresh flat-leaf parsley leaves
2 cloves garlic, peeled
6 ounces turkey breast tenderloin, cubed
1 large egg white
$\frac{1}{4}$ cup freshly squeezed lemon juice
$\frac{1}{4}$ cup diced sweet roasted pepper (see Pantry)
1 tablespoon small capers (nonpareils), drained
$\frac{1}{4}$ cup bread crumbs (see Pantry)
2 tablespoons freshly grated Parmigiano-Reggiano cheese
$1\frac{1}{2}$ cups dry white wine

Steam the artichokes for 20 minutes, then refresh them briefly under cold running water. Set aside.

Preheat the oven to 350 degrees.

In a food processor, finely chop the parsley and garlic. Add the turkey and process until chopped. Remove to a bowl and stir in the egg white, lemon juice, roasted pepper, capers, and 2 tablespoons of the bread crumbs.

Cut each artichoke in half lengthwise. With a spoon or the tip of a sharp knife, remove the hairy chokes and purple leaves, creating a cavity in the center of each half. Mound about $\frac{1}{4}$ cup of the turkey filling in each cavity. Place in a shallow baking dish. Combine the remaining 2 tablespoons bread crumbs and the Parmesan cheese in a small bowl. Sprinkle 1 tablespoon of the cheese mixture over each artichoke half and pour the wine around them.

Cover the pan with aluminum foil and bake for 20 minutes. Remove the foil and bake for about 15 minutes more, until the artichokes are lightly browned, then place them under the broiler for about 4 minutes, until well browned. Place a stuffed artichoke half in each of 4 pasta bowls and spoon the pan juices over them.

Yield = 4 servings
Fat per serving = 0.98 g.
Calories per serving = 158.4

Pork alla Romana

8 ounces green bell pepper (about 1 large pepper), cored, seeded, and cut into strips

8 ounces yellow bell pepper (about 1 large pepper), cored, seeded, and cut into strips

8 ounces yellow onion (about 1 onion), peeled and cut into strips

6 ounces boneless pork loin cutlets, trimmed and cut across the grain into thin strips (about 1/2-by-2 inches)

1 pound tomatoes (about 2 tomatoes), peeled, seeded, and diced (about 1 1/2 cups)

1/2 cup dry white wine

1/4 teaspoon crushed red pepper flakes, or to taste

2 cloves garlic, peeled

1 teaspoon arrowroot dissolved in 1 tablespoon water

Salt to taste

Preheat a large nonstick skillet over high heat. Add the bell peppers and onion and cook for about 4 minutes, stirring constantly, until the vegetables are beginning to brown. Add the pork, tomatoes, wine, and red pepper flakes. Press in the garlic. Sauté until the meat is no longer pink, 1 to 2 minutes. Cover, reduce the heat to medium-low, and simmer until the vegetables are tender and the pork is cooked through, about 10 minutes.

Remove the pan from the heat and stir in the arrowroot mixture. Return to the heat and cook for about 2 minutes more to thicken the sauce. Add salt to taste. Serve a generous 3/4 cup to each person.

Yield = 6 servings
Fat per serving = 0.83 g.
Calories per serving = 82.7

WHEREAS THE original version of the old recipe we updated for this dish calls for the meat to be fried in oil, we simmer it in a mixture of wine and seasonings, which, cooked down and thickened with arrowroot, lends a sheer, silky coating. Speckled with yellow and green bell peppers, the dish is much lighter and more colorful than the typical stew—more like a stir-fry.

Pork alla Romana is good accompanied by Spinach and Roasted Garlic Polenta (page 173) or fettucine made from Carrot Pasta (page 117).

Polenta

(Polenta)

Roasted Pepper and Tomato Tart in a Roasted Polenta Shell ⌒ Herb Polenta ⌒ Spinach and Roasted Garlic Polenta ⌒ Soft Polenta ⌒ Stiff Polenta ⌒ Turkey Lasagne with Polenta ⌒ Mushroom Polenta ⌒ Sun-Dried Tomato Polenta ⌒ Breakfast Polenta

11. *Polenta*

(*Polenta*)

Filling, inexpensive polenta, which sustained Italians through generations of poverty, is now a staple of the country's diet by choice, particularly in the north. Polenta is certainly one of the most versatile of dishes. It can be made soft or stiff, heaped right out of the polenta pot or molded, sliced, and grilled, served as the base for a stew or sauce, as a side dish, as crostini, or even as a little meal by itself.

All those charming stories of old women standing ritualistically for hours stirring heavy cauldrons of polenta over open fires aside, there really is little mystery involved in successful polenta-making. Twenty minutes or so of frequent, not constant, stirring of a cornmeal mixture cooked in any reasonably sturdy saucepan will in fact do the trick.

Polenta is inherently low in fat and can transform a modest serving of a meat-based stew into a hearty meal. It can be made with yellow or white cornmeal; with the coarse Italian cornmeal often imported to the United States, which produces a granular polenta, or with the finer-grained domestic variety, which produces a smoother, more porridgelike polenta; with water or with milk, which enriches it. Each polenta will have a slightly different character, but all are equally good.

In addition to plain soft and stiff polentas, we offer recipes for polenta flavored with sun-dried tomatoes, with spinach and roasted garlic, and with an assortment of herbs. Our sampling includes a rich porcini-accented polenta mounded on portobellos, a medley of roasted peppers and tomatoes served up in a polenta tart, and a lasagne made with layers of polenta rather than noodles, as well as a honeyed breakfast polenta brimming with fruit.

Roasted Pepper and Tomato Tart in a Roasted Polenta Shell

2 pounds mixed red, green, and yellow bell peppers (about 4 large peppers)

1⅓ cups skim milk

¼ cup buttermilk

⅛ teaspoon salt

½ cup coarse yellow Italian cornmeal

Olive oil cooking spray

2 cloves garlic, peeled and very thinly sliced

12 ounces tomatoes (about 2 small tomatoes), peeled, seeded, and chopped (about 1 cup, packed), or 1 cup thoroughly drained canned or boxed tomatoes

½ teaspoon anchovy paste

2 tablespoons chopped fresh flat-leaf parsley

2 tablespoons chopped fresh basil

⅛ to ¼ teaspoon crushed red pepper flakes

2 tablespoons freshly grated Parmigiano-Reggiano cheese (optional)

Preheat the broiler. Line a broiler rack with aluminum foil.

Halve lengthwise, core, and seed the bell peppers. Place them cut side down on the prepared rack, 2 to 3 inches from the heat source. Broil for about 5 minutes, until charred. Remove the rack and turn the oven down to 350 degrees. Seal the peppers in an airtight bag for about 10 minutes, then rub their skins off, slice them thin, and set them aside.

In a small saucepan, combine the skim milk, buttermilk, and salt over medium heat. Slowly whisk in the cornmeal. Reduce the heat to low and cook for about 10 minutes, stirring constantly, until the mixture is smooth and thick enough for a spoonful to hold its shape.

Lightly coat a 13½-by-4½-inch rectangular or 7-inch round tart pan with a removable bottom with olive oil spray. Pour the polenta into the pan and use a rubber spatula to work it up to line the sides. Smooth out the bottom with the back of a wet spoon. Spray again with olive oil. Bake for 5 minutes. Remove from the oven and set aside, leaving the oven on.

Preheat a large nonstick skillet over medium-high heat. Add the garlic and stir a few times until the garlic begins to give off an aroma. Add the tomatoes and roasted peppers. Cook for about 2 minutes, until the mixture becomes dry. Stir in the anchovy paste, parsley, basil, and crushed red pepper to taste. Cook and stir for about 1 minute to heat through and allow the flavors to blend.

Pour the mixture into the polenta shell. Bake for about 15 minutes, until the edges are just starting to brown, then place under the broiler for about 5 minutes, until well browned. Remove to a rack and cool for 10 minutes.

If desired, sprinkle with Parmesan cheese before cutting and serving.

Yield = 6 servings
Fat per serving = 0.59 g.
Calories per serving = 94.9

Herb Polenta

This delicate polenta is best molded and then broiled or grilled in slices. It is made of white cornmeal in the fashion of Veneto, one of those northern Italian regions where cornmeal is so popular that the inhabitants are sometimes called "polenta eaters." Herb Polenta goes well with almost any simple tomato sauce, such as Tomato-Mint Sauce (page 128), as well as with Meat Sauce (page 126), Mushroom Sauce (page 127), or Spicy Roasted Garlic and Eggplant Sauce (page 125).

2 cups buttermilk
1½ cups Chicken Stock (see page 19)
1 cup fine white cornmeal
1 tablespoon chopped fresh flat-leaf parsley
1 tablespoon chopped fresh basil

½ tablespoon chopped fresh oregano
½ tablespoon chopped fresh thyme
1 tablespoon freshly grated Parmigiano-Reggiano cheese
⅛ teaspoon freshly ground black pepper

Combine the buttermilk and stock in a medium saucepan over medium heat. Whisking occasionally, bring to a boil. While whisking, add the cornmeal in a thin stream. Reduce the heat to medium-low and cook, stirring frequently, until the polenta easily pulls away from the sides of the pan and a spoon pulled through it leaves a clean track, about 15 minutes.

Remove the pan from the heat and stir in the parsley, basil, oregano, and thyme. Stir in the Parmesan and black pepper.

To mold, scrape into a nonstick 8-inch loaf pan, cover, and refrigerate for 2 hours.

Remove the polenta loaf from the pan and cut it into eight 1-inch slices. Broil or grill them for 2 to 3 minutes per side, until well browned.

Yield = 8 servings
Fat per serving = 0.88 g.
Calories per serving = 90.9

Spinach and Roasted Garlic Polenta

10 ounces fresh spinach (about 4 cups)

4 large cloves roasted garlic (see Pantry)

5 cups Vegetable Stock (see page 20)

1½ cups coarse yellow Italian cornmeal

2 tablespoons Pecorino Toscano cheese

Preheat a medium saucepan over high heat. Rinse the spinach and place it in the pan with the water still clinging to the leaves. Cook, stirring, until the spinach is thoroughly wilted, 2 to 3 minutes. Remove the spinach to the bowl of a food processor or blender, add the roasted garlic, and puree. Set aside.

Bring the stock to a boil in a medium saucepan over high heat. Slowly add the cornmeal while whisking. Reduce the heat to medium and continue to cook, stirring frequently, until the polenta easily pulls away from the sides of the pan and mounds on the back of a spoon, 18 to 20 minutes. Stir in the puree and the cheese.

To mold, scrape into a nonstick 9½-inch loaf pan, cover, and refrigerate for 2 hours.

Remove the polenta loaf from the pan and cut it into twelve ¾-inch slices. Broil or grill them for 2 to 3 minutes per side, until well browned. Serve 2 slices to each person.

Yield = 6 servings
Fat per serving = 0.95 g.
Calories per serving = 162.4

SPINACH AND ROASTED Garlic Polenta is quite robust enough to serve on its own hot out of the pot, but it also complements Pork alla Romana (page 165) or Raw Tomato Sauce (page 130) when molded and broiled or grilled. We top this dish with a bit of Pecorino Toscano, which is softer and richer-tasting than the more familiar Pecorino Romano—more of a cross between Pecorino Romano and Parmesan cheese.

Soft Polenta

Soft Polenta makes a wonderful base for stews and sauced dishes of all sorts. We serve it with Turkey with Mushrooms, Zucchini, and Fennel (page 160), with Monkfish Osso Buco (page138), with Meat Sauce (page 126), and with Spicy Roasted Garlic and Eggplant Sauce (page 125). This recipe calls for the kind of coarse-grained Italian cornmeal that is often referred to simply as "polenta," especially in Italian markets. Unlike molded and chilled polentas, the soft variety does not hold up well and should be made at the same time as the dish that will top it.

6½ cups water
2 cups coarse yellow Italian cornmeal
1 tablespoon freshly grated
  Parmigiano-Reggiano cheese

¼ teaspoon freshly ground black
  pepper

In a large saucepan over high heat, bring the water to a boil.

While whisking constantly, add the cornmeal in a thin stream and bring back to a boil. Reduce the heat to low and cook, stirring frequently, for 20 to 30 minutes, until very thick (the polenta pulls away from the sides of the pan when stirred) and creamy. Stir in the Parmesan and pepper.

Yield = 6 servings
Fat per serving = 0.90 g.
Calories per serving = 172.7

Stiff Polenta

1⅓ cups skim milk
¼ cup buttermilk
½ teaspoon sugar
⅛ teaspoon salt

½ cup fine yellow cornmeal
2 cloves garlic, peeled
Olive oil cooking spray

Combine the skim milk, buttermilk, sugar, and salt in a small saucepan over medium heat. Slowly whisk in the cornmeal. Reduce the heat to low and cook, stirring constantly, for about 5 minutes, until the mixture is thick and smooth and comes away easily from the sides of the pan. Press in the garlic.

Spray a 5¾-inch mini loaf pan lightly with the olive oil and rub the oil over the surface to coat. Scrape the cornmeal mixture into the pan, cover, and chill for at least 1 hour in the refrigerator.

Remove the polenta loaf from the pan and cut it into six scant inch-thick slices. Broil or grill them for 2 to 3 minutes per side, until well browned.

Yield = 6 servings
Fat per serving = 0.38 g.
Calories per serving = 67.8

WE USE THIS PLAIN, molded polenta as a foil for such robust dishes as Turkey alla Cacciatora (page 162) and Baby Octopus Ragù (page 140)—or with a simple splash of Mushroom Sauce (page 127) or Tomato-Oregano Sauce (page 131). Many Italians simply turn the polenta out onto a cutting board and cut it with a taut string, but you may want to practice a bit before trying that approach. We suggest molding it in a loaf pan and then using a good knife instead.

Turkey Lasagne with Polenta

Here is an Italian solution to a perennial American problem. This one-of-a-kind lasagne, layered with rich, creamy polenta instead of noodles, will make Thanksgiving leftovers disappear quickly! The rest of the year, start with a piece of oven-roasted turkey breast from your supermarket's poultry section. Look for *real* turkey breast on the bone rather than for the more common pressed turkey.

This lasagne is a good party dish—it feeds a crowd, holds up on a buffet, and keeps well for days in the refrigerator.

6¾ cups water

1 tablespoon plus ¼ teaspoon salt

2 cups fine yellow cornmeal

10 ounces yellow onion (about 1 large onion), chopped (about 1¾ cups)

2 large cloves garlic, chopped

3 cups cut-up canned or boxed tomatoes with their juice

¼ teaspoon crushed red pepper flakes

One 15-ounce container skim-milk ricotta cheese

½ cup nonfat liquid egg substitute

⅛ teaspoon freshly ground black pepper

9 ounces cooked turkey breast, shredded (about 1½ cups)

1 teaspoon dried basil

2 tablespoons freshly grated Parmigiano-Reggiano cheese

Bring 6½ cups of the water to a boil in a large saucepan over high heat. Add 1 tablespoon of the salt. While whisking, add the cornmeal in a thin stream. Bring back to a boil, whisking constantly. Reduce the heat to low and cook for about 20 minutes, stirring frequently, until very thick (thick enough for a spoonful to hold its shape) and creamy. Spread about half to cover the bottom of a 9-by-13-inch nonstick baking dish and refrigerate for about 20 minutes to firm, keeping the remainder warm over low heat.

Meanwhile, combine the onion and the remaining ¼ cup water in a large nonstick skillet over medium heat. Cook for about 5 minutes, until the onion is just beginning to color. Stir in the garlic and cook until it begins to give off an aroma, about 30 seconds. Add the tomatoes, along with the red pepper flakes. Cook for about 30 minutes more, stirring periodically, until most of the liquid has been absorbed and the mixture can be easily mashed with the back of a spoon.

While the tomatoes cook, combine the ricotta cheese, egg substitute, black pepper, and the remaining ¼ teaspoon salt in a medium bowl and mix thoroughly.

Preheat the oven to 400 degrees.

Remove the baking dish from the refrigerator and spread half of the ricotta cheese mixture (a generous cup) on top of the chilled polenta. Add the turkey and basil to the tomato mixture and layer it over the ricotta cheese. Top with the remaining ricotta and then the remaining polenta, dropped over the cheese in small mounds and spread to smooth it. Sprinkle with the Parmesan cheese.

Bake in the middle of the oven for about 35 minutes, until browned around the edges. Remove to a wire rack and cool for 20 minutes before cutting into twelve 3-by-3¼-inch slices.

Yield = 12 servings
Fat per serving = 0.83 g.
Calories per serving = 165.7

Mushroom Polenta

CREAMY CORNMEAL luxuriously laced with porcinis and freshly grated Parmigiano-Reggiano sits in mounds atop hearty portobellos in this mushroom lover's delight. Since fresh porcini mushrooms are rare in the United States, we use dried porcinis that have been reconstituted.

½ cup dried porcini mushrooms
1½ cups hot tap water
2 cups Beef Stock (see page 21)
1 cup fine yellow cornmeal
⅛ teaspoon freshly grated black
  pepper

6 ounces portobello mushrooms
  (about four 4-inch mushrooms),
  trimmed and cleaned
2 teaspoons freshly grated
  Parmigiano-Reggiano cheese

Combine the dried porcini mushrooms and the water in a small bowl. Set aside for 15 minutes to reconstitute. Remove the mushrooms and squeeze them dry. Add water as needed to the reconstituting liquid to equal 1½ cups.

Preheat the broiler.

In a medium saucepan, bring the reconstituting liquid and the stock to a boil over high heat. Slowly add the cornmeal while whisking. Reduce the heat to medium and cook, stirring frequently, for 10 minutes. Stir in the porcini mushrooms. Continue to cook, stirring frequently, until thick enough for a spoonful to hold its shape, about 10 minutes more. Stir in the black pepper.

Meanwhile, place the portobello mushrooms on a microwave-safe plate, cover loosely, and microwave at full power until soft and beginning to give off steam, about 1 minute. Remove the mushrooms to a broiler tray, stem side up, top each with a generous ½ cup of polenta, and sprinkle with ½ teaspoon of the Parmesan. Position 5 inches from the heat source and broil for about 4 minutes, until the cheese has melted and the top is brown.

Yield = 4 servings
Fat per serving = 0.90 g.
Calories per serving = 162.5

Sun-Dried Tomato Polenta

1 ounce sun-dried tomatoes (about 10 to 12 tomatoes)
½ cup boiling water
2 cups tap water

1 cup buttermilk
½ teaspoon salt
½ teaspoon sugar
1 cup fine yellow or white cornmeal

Combine the sun-dried tomatoes and the boiling water in a small bowl and let soak for 30 minutes. Drain and chop the tomatoes. (You should have about ⅓ cup chopped tomatoes.)

Combine the tap water, buttermilk, salt, and sugar in a medium saucepan. Bring to a boil over medium-high heat. Reduce the heat to low and whisk in the cornmeal in a thin stream. Cook for 5 to 6 minutes, stirring frequently, until a spoon pulled through the polenta leaves a clean track. Stir in the sun-dried tomatoes and cook for 30 seconds more.

To mold, scrape into a nonstick 8-inch loaf pan, cover, and refrigerate for 2 hours.

Remove the polenta loaf from the pan and cut it into six 1⅓-inch slices. Broil or grill them for 2 to 3 minutes per side, until well browned.

Yield = 6 servings
Fat per serving = 0.78 g.
Calories per serving = 111.9

WE CREATED THIS refined polenta with Quail Ragù (page 156) in mind; it pairs with it wonderfully. Mold the polenta, then slice and broil or grill it. Broiled or grilled, it can also be finished with Yellow Pepper–Mushroom Sauce (page 132). The polenta can be served hot right out of the pot (which does not have to be the copper *paiolo* of Italian tradition—any reasonably heavy pot will do, in which form it is particularly suited to our Meat Sauce (page 126). This recipe can be made with either yellow or white cornmeal; using the latter will make the red flecks of sun-dried tomato stand out especially dramatically.

Breakfast Polenta

We tend to think of polenta as an accompaniment for savory dishes, but it does not have to be. Sweetened with honey and chockful of fruit, polenta makes an intriguing alternative to oatmeal on the breakfast table. We particularly like the apricot-and-blueberry combination featured in this recipe, but let your own taste buds lead the way. Sturdy dried fruit can be added to impart flavor as the polenta cooks, while the more delicate fresh fruit is better spooned on just before serving.

2 cups skim milk
2 cups water
½ teaspoon salt
1 cup fine white or yellow cornmeal

3 ounces dried apricots, chopped
   (about ½ cup)
3 tablespoons honey
½ pint blueberries, picked over

In a small saucepan, scald the milk over medium heat just until bubbles form around the edge, about 3 minutes.

Combine the water and salt in a medium saucepan and bring to a boil. Reduce the heat to low and while whisking, add the cornmeal in a continuous slow stream. Add the milk in thirds, whisking after each addition. Continue to cook, whisking frequently, until the polenta is as thick as oatmeal and clumps around the wires of the whisk, about 10 minutes.

Add the apricots. Stir in 1 tablespoon of the honey with a wooden spoon. (The polenta will by now have become too dense to whisk.) Cook for about 5 minutes more, until the polenta is so thick that a spoonful raised above the pan will cling to the back of the spoon. Serve a generous 1 cup to each person. Combine the blueberries and the remaining 2 tablespoons honey and spoon 2 heaping tablespoons of the mixture over each serving.

Yield = 4 servings
Fat per serving = 0.93 g.
Calories per serving = 287.5

Vegetables

(Contorni)

Italian Potatoes with Onion and Rosemary ⁓ Simmered Greens ⁓ Rapini with Red Pepper ⁓ Garlic Custard ⁓ Baked Eggplant and Cheese ⁓ Lemon-Garlic Broccoli ⁓ Eggplant Fritters ⁓ Baked Artichokes ⁓ Cauliflower Italian Style ⁓ Kale Wilted in Balsamic Vinegar

12. *Vegetables*

(Contorni)

The same factors that dictated the limited use of meat in Italian cooking—geography and economics—prompted an abundance of vegetable dishes. The Italian climate is such that an amazing array of fresh, inexpensive vegetables is always readily available.

The markets in Italy are equaled by few others we've seen. Wandering among the stalls, we quickly discovered that our American custom of shopping with a list reflecting some predetermined menu is not the best approach. Food this fresh and flavorful should dictate what the meal will be.

The Italians cook vegetables well in a variety of ways. In our sampling, we focus on the simplest of stovetop methods—simmering rapini and greens, steaming cauliflower, sautéing eggplant and potatoes, and wilting kale, usually using wine, sometimes water, a spritz of olive oil only when absolutely necessary. (Today's nonstick surfaces allow amazing results without the use of oil.) Broccoli we first boil and then finish briefly in a lemon-garlic mixture over high heat. A few dishes, including a silky garlic flan and a hearty eggplant casserole, are baked, as are artichokes, an Italian favorite.

Italian Potatoes with Onion and Rosemary

2¼ pounds baking potatoes (about 4
  potatoes), scrubbed, peeled, and
  thinly sliced (about 4 cups)
10 ounces yellow onion (about 1 large
  onion), peeled and thinly sliced
  (about 1¾ cups)
2 cloves garlic, chopped

⅓ cup dry white wine
2 tablespoons chopped fresh flat-leaf
  parsley
2 teaspoons chopped fresh rosemary
Salt and freshly ground black pepper
  to taste

Cook the potatoes in a microwave oven at full power for 7 to 8 minutes,
until fork-tender. (You can also boil the potatoes for 30 to 35 minutes in
4 cups of water to which 2 teaspoons of salt have been added.) Set the
potatoes aside until cool enough to handle.

Preheat a large nonstick skillet over medium-low heat. In the hot skillet,
combine the onion, garlic, and wine. Stir to combine thoroughly and cook
for about 15 minutes, until the onion is very soft.

Add the potatoes, parsley, and rosemary. Mix well and mash with the back
of a wooden spoon to form a large pancake. Season with salt and pepper to
taste. Raise the heat to medium and cook for about 15 minutes, until the
potatoes are browned and somewhat crusty underneath. Position a plate
upside down over the pan, flip the pancake out onto the plate so that the
cooked side is up, and then slide it back into the pan. Cook for about
15 minutes more, until the second side is crusty.

Yield = 4 servings
Fat per serving = 0.44 g.
Calories per serving = 327.5

Simmered Greens

1 pound mustard greens, cleaned,
 stemmed, and sliced crosswise
1 clove garlic, minced

¼ cup white wine
Salt and freshly ground black pepper
 to taste

Preheat a large, nonstick skillet over medium heat. Add the greens, garlic, and wine. Cover and cook for about 15 minutes, until the greens are wilted and tender. Season with salt and pepper to taste.

Yield = 4 servings
Fat per serving = 0.20 g.
Calories per serving = 40.8

THIS IS AN EXTREMELY simple and satisfying dish. Much like Italian wild greens, these can be served warm or at room temperature as a salad. As a salad, we like to pair the greens with slices of toasted baguette topped with White Bean Spread (page 38). Small portions of greens can also be served on toast as antipasti.

Rapini with Red Pepper

ALSO CALLED *broccoletti di rapa,* or broccoli raab in English, rapini is a lot more robust than plain broccoli and can definitely stand up to the addition of pungent red pepper flakes. Chinese broccoli, which has a similarly bitter bite, can be used interchangeably in this recipe.

1 pound rapini
6 ounces yellow onion (about 1 onion), thinly sliced (about 1 cup)
2 large cloves garlic, roughly chopped
1/8 teaspoon crushed red pepper flakes, or to taste

1/2 cup dry white wine
1 tablespoon freshly squeezed lemon juice

Cut away any yellow or wilted leaves from the rapini and trim the ends. Peel any thick stems with a paring knife or vegetable peeler. Cut the leaves and stems into 2-inch pieces.

Preheat a large nonstick skillet over medium heat. Scatter the onion in a thin layer over the bottom. Add the rapini in as thin a layer as possible. Scatter the garlic and red pepper flakes over the rapini. Add the wine. Cover and cook for about 15 minutes, until the wine has evaporated and the rapini is fork-tender. Sprinkle with the lemon juice just before serving.

Yield = 4 servings
Fat per serving = 0.33 g.
Calories per serving = 60.3

Garlic Custard

Olive oil cooking spray
1 cup buttermilk
2 teaspoons all-purpose flour
½ cup evaporated skim milk
1 large bay leaf

2 sprigs flat-leaf parsley
2 sprigs rosemary
6 large cloves garlic
1 cup nonfat liquid egg substitute
2 to 3 cups boiling water

Preheat the oven to 375 degrees. Spray each of four 4-ounce ramekins once with the cooking spray.

In a small bowl, whisk together the buttermilk and flour.

Combine the buttermilk mixture, evaporated milk, bay leaf, parsley, and rosemary in a small saucepan. Press in the garlic. Cook over medium heat for about 5 minutes, stirring constantly, until the mixture is steaming vigorously and the garlic has just begun to become aromatic. Remove the bay leaf, parsley, and rosemary and whisk in the liquid egg substitute.

Divide the custard mixture equally among the prepared ramekins, place them in a baking dish, and fill the dish with boiling water to come halfway up the sides of the ramekins. Bake for about 30 minutes, until the custard is puffy and firm. Remove the ramekins from the pan and cool the custards for 5 minutes. Run a knife around the inner edge of each ramekin to loosen the custard. Invert and gently top the ramekin bottom to release the custard onto the desired serving plate.

Yield = 4 servings
Fat per serving = 0.54 g.
Calories per serving = 84.5

THE HEADY AROMA and pungent taste of garlic become even more intoxicating in the form of a delicate custard. This makes a nice accompaniment to entrees with tomato-based sauces, such as Quail Ragù (page 156) and Turkey alla Cacciatora (page 162). It's also rather elegant served on a salad base. Try the custard on a bed of dandelion greens, topped with the balsamic-vinegar-and-orange dressing we use to dress our Fava Bean and Dandelion Green Salad (page 199).

Baked Eggplant and Cheese

THIS IS OUR healthful update of the ubiquitous eggplant parmigiana, in which we bake the eggplant rounds to get the crisp, golden exterior usually achieved by frying them in oil and we substitute skim-milk feta cheese for the traditional whole-milk mozzarella. This can be served as a side dish or as a light vegetarian main course for 4.

Olive oil cooking spray

1½ pounds purple eggplant (about 1 medium eggplant), trimmed and cut into ½-inch-thick rounds

Salt and freshly ground black pepper to taste

7 ounces yellow onion (about 1 onion), chopped (about 1 cup)

¼ cup dry white wine

4 large cloves garlic, chopped

3 cups canned crushed tomatoes

1 tablespoon chopped fresh basil, plus additional for garnish

4 ounces skim-milk feta cheese, crumbled (about ¾ cup)

Preheat the oven to 475 degrees. Spray a large baking sheet lightly with the olive oil.

Arrange the eggplant in a single layer on the prepared sheet. Spray again lightly with olive oil. Sprinkle with salt and pepper. Bake for about 20 minutes, until tender and lightly browned, turning the eggplant rounds over after 10 minutes. Remove from the oven and lower the temperature to 350 degrees.

Preheat a medium nonstick skillet over medium-high heat. Add the onion and wine. Cook and stir for about 2 minutes, until the onion begins to brown. Stir in the garlic, tomatoes, and basil. Add salt and pepper to taste. Reduce the heat to medium and simmer for about 20 minutes, until the sauce has thickened and reduced by about a third.

Ladle about 1 cup of the sauce into a shallow 11-by-7-inch baking dish. Add the eggplant rounds, overlapping them slightly. Top with the remaining sauce. Sprinkle the feta cheese over the casserole.

Bake for about 20 minutes, until heated through, then remove from the oven and let sit for 5 minutes. Garnish with a sprinkling of chopped basil before serving.

Yield = 6 servings
Fat per serving = 0.55 g.
Calories per serving = 107.3

Lemon-Garlic Broccoli

1 teaspoon salt

1 pound broccoli, cut into long-stemmed florets

2 tablespoons freshly squeezed lemon juice

1 large clove garlic, chopped

BOILING VEGETABLES and then finishing them in a skillet with seasonings is a classic Italian preparation. Here we season simply with a squeeze of lemon juice and a clove of garlic. We prefer to start with a whole head of broccoli so we can retain some stem on the florets, but you could easily start with precut florets if you are pressed for time.

Fill a Dutch oven halfway with water and bring to a boil over high heat. Add the salt, then the broccoli. Boil for about 5 minutes, until crisp-tender. Drain, reserving ¼ cup of the cooking water. Put the broccoli in a colander, rinse it briefly under cold running water, and set it aside to drain.

In a small bowl, mix together the lemon juice, garlic, and reserved broccoli water.

Preheat a large nonstick skillet over high heat. Add the broccoli and the lemon juice mixture. Tossing occasionally, cook for about 2 minutes, until the water has evaporated and the broccoli is heated through.

Yield = 4 servings
Fat per serving = 0.26 g.
Calories per serving = 23.3

Eggplant Fritters

Eggplant slices fried to just the right consistency—crisp on the outside and soft inside—are always a favorite. In this case, the "frying" is done in a nonstick pan sprayed ever so lightly with olive oil. A mandoline yields the very thin slices of eggplant that will work best. For an even crisper coating, use 2 large egg whites beaten with 2 tablespoons of water instead of the egg substitute in the batter.

1 pound purple eggplant (about 1 small eggplant)
1 teaspoon coarse salt
1/4 cup nonfat liquid egg substitute
2 tablespoons all-purpose flour
1 tablespoon water
Olive oil cooking spray

Cut the eggplant in half lengthwise, sprinkle it with the salt, and set it aside for 45 minutes. Pat the eggplant dry with paper towels and slice it very thin lengthwise.

In a wide, shallow bowl, whisk together the egg substitute, flour, and water. Dip the eggplant slices in the batter to coat them all over.

Preheat a large nonstick skillet over medium-high heat; spray it once with the olive oil. Cook the eggplant in batches for about 1 minute, until the tops look dry and the bottoms are browned. Flip and cook for about 1 minute more, until browned on the second side.

Yield = 6 servings
Fat per serving = 0.11 g.
Calories per serving = 28.6

Baked Artichokes

Two large artichokes (10 to 12 ounces each)
½ large lemon

1 tablespoon capers, drained
3 large cloves garlic, peeled
¾ cup Vegetable Stock (see page 20)

Preheat the oven to 500 degrees.

Cut the stem of each artichoke flush with the base and clip the sharp point at the tip of each leaf with scissors. Cut each artichoke in half lengthwise and remove the hairy chokes with a spoon or the tip of a sharp knife. Rub the cut sides with the lemon. Place the artichokes cut side down in a baking dish. Scatter the capers and garlic over them and add ½ cup of the stock. Cover the dish with aluminum foil and bake the artichokes for about 45 minutes, until fork-tender at the stem end.

Remove the artichokes to shallow bowls. Pour the remaining contents of the baking dish into a food processor or blender. Add the remaining ¼ cup stock and puree. Pour the sauce over the artichokes.

Yield = 4 servings
Fat per serving = 0.06 g.
Calories per serving = 22.1

AFTER YEARS OF steaming artichokes, we recently discovered just how good they are baked. Whereas the sauce is typically something to dip artichoke leaves into and is usually an afterthought, baking allows you to cook the artichokes in the sauce (in this case a broth redolent of garlic and capers). As the artichokes cook, they are permeated with the sauce, becoming particularly flavorful and aromatic.

Cauliflower Italian Style

In this basic preparation, cauliflower is first steamed with garlic, then tossed with capers, parsley, and Parmesan cheese. Cauliflower is more traditionally flavored with either olives or anchovies, but we rather like the touch the capers provide. Large capers have a more assertive flavor than the smaller nonpareils; for a milder-tasting dish or to avoid chopping, use small capers whole.

2 pounds cauliflower, trimmed and cut into 1-inch florets (about 8 cups)
2 large cloves garlic, chopped
⅓ cup water
2 tablespoons chopped fresh flat-leaf parsley

1 tablespoon capers, drained and roughly chopped
2 teaspoons freshly grated Parmigiano-Reggiano cheese

Preheat a large nonstick skillet over medium heat. Add the cauliflower, garlic, and water. Cover and cook for about 10 minutes, until all the water has evaporated and the cauliflower is fork-tender. Uncover and add the parsley, capers, and Parmesan. Stir and cook for another minute or two to heat through.

Yield = 6 servings
Fat per serving = 0.19 g.
Calories per serving = 19.8

Kale Wilted in Balsamic Vinegar

12 ounces kale (about 1 bunch), stemmed and chopped (about 8 cups)

2 large cloves garlic, chopped
1/4 cup water
1/4 cup balsamic vinegar

Preheat a large, nonstick skillet over medium heat. Add the kale, garlic, water, and vinegar. Cover and cook for 7 to 8 minutes, until all the liquid has been absorbed and the kale is tender.

Yield = 4 servings
Fat per serving = 0.36 g.
Calories per serving = 28.7

ALTHOUGH IT'S RARE to find Italian recipes for kale—which can be found in Tuscany but seldom elsewhere—we include this dish for several reasons. Kale is exceptionally healthful and low in fat, it's quick and easy to prepare, and it takes well to some of the most intrinsically Italian flavorings, namely garlic and balsamic vinegar.

As Americans come increasingly to appreciate kale, we're finally learning how to cook it right—steamed for just a few minutes, instead of cooked seemingly for days.

Salads

(Insalate)

Grilled Calamari and White Bean Salad ⌒ Fava Bean and Dandelion Green Salad ⌒ Arugula Salad with Apple and Bacon ⌒ Seafood and Rice Salad with Pesto ⌒ Celeriac Slaw ⌒ Orange-Fennel Salad ⌒ Roasted Eggplant and Fennel Salad ⌒ Bean and Tomato Salad ⌒ Tuscan Bread Salad ⌒ Orzo Salad with Capers and Tomatoes ⌒ Roasted Pear and Frisée Salad

13. Salads

(Insalate)

Once upon a time, Italian salads were mostly green and served at the end of the meal. Salads worldwide are chameleon-like today. They may be served after dinner, before the main course, as an accompaniment, or as the meal. A recipe that yields a side salad (whenever it might be served) for 4 could be luncheon fare or a light supper for 2, or even the main meal for one hungry diner.

Salads are fun, they're healthful, and within reason they're very open to transformation. The only thing traditional about our salads is the use of elements familiar in the Italian kitchen: arugula and radicchio; fennel; basil, parsley, oregano, and thyme; eggplant, peppers, and tomatoes; fruit; white beans and fava beans; calamari, mussels, scallops, and shrimp; rice, pasta, and bread. Like modern Italians, we put them together in ever-changing configurations.

Since the dictates of fat-free cooking preclude the use of the classic Italian olive oil dressing, we use sparing amounts of simple citrus mixtures, balsamic vinegar mixtures, vinaigrettes thickened with corn syrup, or pestos made with pasta or rice cooking liquid instead of with oil.

Grilled Calamari and White Bean Salad

In this elegant and colorful recipe, pale grilled squid and cannellini beans, the latter dotted with flecks of sun-dried tomato, rest on a mound of red radicchio. In Italy, a number of greens share the label *radicchio*, from the leafy Treviso variety, the most acclaimed, to heads of Chioggia, which is the kind that is shipped to the rest of the world. Although some folks search out small heads in the belief that they will be younger and tenderer, the teacher and author Marcella Hazan has pointed out that since all heads are about the same size, the supposed babies are in fact old heads from which the greengrocer has plucked the outer leaves, no longer in their prime.

4 large cleaned squid bodies (about 4 ounces)
1/4 cup freshly squeezed lemon juice
1 teaspoon chopped fresh oregano
4 cloves garlic, peeled
1/4 cup chopped sun-dried tomatoes
1/4 cup water

3 cups cooked cannellini beans (see Pantry)
2 tablespoons chopped fresh flat-leaf parsley
1/2 teaspoon chopped fresh oregano
4 ounces radicchio (about 1 small head), shredded (about 1 cup)

Cut the squid in half lengthwise. Score each piece with two diagonal slashes in each direction to form a crosshatch. In a nonreactive mixing bowl, combine the lemon juice and oregano. Press in 2 cloves of the garlic. Add the squid and marinate for 15 minutes.

Meanwhile, preheat a stovetop grill or the oven broiler.

Combine the sun-dried tomatoes and the water in a small microwave-safe bowl. Cover loosely and microwave at full power for about 1 minute to re-constitute the tomatoes. (You can also reconstitute the tomatoes by combining them with enough boiling water to cover and letting them steep until soft, 20 to 30 minutes.) In another mixing bowl, combine the beans, parsley, and oregano. Press in the remaining 2 cloves garlic. Drain the reconstituted tomatoes and add them to the bean mixture.

Grill or broil the squid for 25 to 30 seconds per side, until opaque and lightly browned.

On each of 4 salad plates, mound 1/4 cup of the shredded radicchio. Top with 3/4 cup of the bean mixture and 2 pieces of squid.

Yield = 4 servings
Fat per serving = 0.89 g.
Calories per serving = 202.9

Fava Bean and Dandelion Green Salad

4 cups water

¼ teaspoon salt, plus additional to taste

1 pound fava beans, shelled

6 ounces dandelion greens, stemmed, rinsed, dried, and cut into 1½-inch pieces

8 ounces tomato (about 1 tomato), cored, seeded, and chopped (about 1 cup)

3 tablespoons chopped Vidalia onion

DRESSING:

¼ cup balsamic vinegar

1 tablespoon freshly squeezed orange juice

2 tablespoons chopped fresh flat-leaf parsley

1 tablespoon sun-dried tomato paste

Freshly ground black pepper to taste

In a medium saucepan, bring the water to a boil over high heat. Add the ¼ teaspoon salt and the fava beans. Cook for 30 seconds, drain, and rinse under cold water. Peel the beans.

In a salad bowl, combine the fava beans, dandelion greens, tomato, and onion.

For the dressing, combine the vinegar, orange juice, parsley, and tomato paste in a small bowl. Add salt and black pepper generously to taste. Mix well, pour over the vegetables, and toss to coat.

Serve 1 cup to each person.

Yield = 4 servings
Fat per serving: 0.57 g.
Calories per serving: 61.3

ON A RECENT TREK through rural Illinois in search of morels, we kept encountering an older couple harvesting something that was obviously not mushrooms. We finally just had to ask, only to learn that they were picking wild dandelion greens. Intrigued, we decided to make a salad combining some of these slightly bitter greens with our favorite vegetable, fava beans. To balance the flavors, we added some sweet Vidalia onions, which come to market in the spring at about the same time as fava beans.

Fava beans are a bit labor-intensive, because you must first remove the beans from their pods and then, unless the beans are very young, peel off the skins—a task made much easier by blanching the beans after shelling them. Given that they are wonderful eaten right out of the shell, the biggest problem becomes mustering enough self-discipline not to consume them as fast as you skin them.

This salad is finished much as a spinach salad is: dressed in a sweet vinaigrette and sprinkled with crumbled bacon. The main ingredient, however, is not spinach but the much more assertive, peppery arugula, tempered with a bit of apple. Look for tender baby arugula leaves. Don't be put off by our seemingly quirky use of maple syrup in the dressing. You won't taste the syrup once the dressing is mixed; it merely sweetens and coats, much as oil would.

Arugula Salad with Apple and Bacon

2 strips turkey bacon
2 tablespoons balsamic vinegar
2 tablespoons pure maple syrup
3 ounces arugula, stemmed

7 ounces Gala apple (about 1 apple), cored and cut into 1-inch cubes (about 1⅓ cups)

Preheat the oven to 400 degrees. Line a baking dish with aluminum foil.

Place the bacon in the prepared dish and bake for 14 to 15 minutes, until crisp. Let it cool and cut it into ½-inch pieces (about 2 tablespoons).

Meanwhile, for the dressing, whisk the vinegar and maple syrup together in a small bowl.

Combine the arugula and apple in a mixing bowl, add the dressing, and toss well. Mound 1 cup of the mixture on each of 4 salad plates and top each with ½ tablespoon bacon.

Yield = 4 servings
Fat per serving = 0.68 g.
Calories per serving = 77.4

Seafood and Rice Salad with Pesto

4 cups water

Salt to taste

1 cup Arborio rice

4 ounces bay scallops

1 cup packed fresh basil leaves

1 clove garlic, peeled

1 teaspoon plus 1 tablespoon freshly squeezed lemon juice

4 ounces cooked, peeled medium shrimp, halved

4 ounces cooked, shelled mussels (see sidebar)

4 ounces yellow cherry tomatoes, halved

¾ teaspoon freshly ground black pepper

6 radicchio leaves

In a medium saucepan, bring the 4 cups of water to a boil. Add a pinch of salt and the rice. Cook over medium-high heat for 8 to 10 minutes, until the rice is tender but still firm. Drain well and transfer the rice to a large serving bowl, reserving 6 tablespoons of the cooking liquid.

Fill a medium saucepan halfway with water and bring to a boil over medium-high heat. Add the scallops and cook for 2 minutes, until opaque.

For the pesto, combine the basil, garlic, and 1 teaspoon of the lemon juice in a food processor. Process until roughly chopped. Add the reserved cooking liquid and continue to process until the mixture is smooth.

Add 2 tablespoons of pesto to the rice and toss. Add the scallops, shrimp, mussels, and cherry tomatoes. Add the remaining pesto, the black pepper, 1 tablespoon lemon juice, and salt to taste. Mix well and chill thoroughly.

Place a radicchio leaf on each of 6 plates and divide the seafood salad equally. You should have a generous ¾ cup per serving.

Yield = 6 servings
Fat per serving = 0.99 g.
Calories per serving = 172.3

THIS ABUNDANT FEAST from the sea features shrimp, mussels, and scallops tossed with Arborio rice in a basil-garlic sauce and served on radicchio leaves. It is quicker to prepare if you use green-lip mussels from New Zealand, which are sold frozen, since they are already cleaned and cooked and need only to be scooped out of their shells.

If you use blue mussels, first rinse them under cold running water, discarding any that don't close when tapped or that have broken shells. Put the mussels in a Dutch oven or large saucepan, add about ½ inch of water or white wine, cover, and steam for 5 to 6 minutes. They should open naturally as they cook; discard any that don't.

Celeriac Slaw

HERE WE PAIR CELERY with celeriac, which has an emphatic flavor that lends the celery a whole new character. Dressed in a creamy, garlicky ricotta mixture, it's a bit evocative of a rémoulade. The quickest and easiest way to prepare the celeriac is to use a mandoline fitted with the shoestring attachment. Some metal mandolines we've seen are rather cumbersome and expensive gadgets, but we've been dependent for years on an inexpensive, lightweight plastic model that comes apart for easy storage. It makes quick work of cutting matchsticks, slicing paper thin, and other such tasks.

Use either our homemade Dried Seasoning Blend or prepared Italian seasoning from your supermarket's spice section.

12 ounces celeriac (celery root), trimmed, peeled, and cut into thin matchsticks
6 ounces celery (about 2 stalks), trimmed and cut into ¼-inch cubes (about ⅔ cup)
½ cup diced red bell pepper
¼ cup skim-milk ricotta cheese

1 clove garlic, peeled
1 teaspoon Dried Seasoning Blend (page 22)
1 tablespoon Pecorino Romano cheese
2 tablespoons skim milk
Salt and freshly ground black pepper to taste

Combine the celeriac, celery, and bell pepper in a salad bowl.

In the bowl of a food processor, combine the ricotta cheese, garlic, seasoning, and Pecorino Romano cheese. Turn the machine on and drizzle the milk through the feed tube. Process until smooth, about 1 minute. Pour over the vegetables and toss to coat. Add salt and pepper to taste.

Serve ⅔ cup to each person.

Yield = 6 servings
Fat per serving = 0.55 g.
Calories per serving = 47.0

Orange-Fennel Salad

12 ounces fennel (about 1 bulb), trimmed and sliced very thin (about 2 cups)

½ cup thinly sliced red onion

6 ounces temple oranges (about 2 oranges), peeled and sectioned (about ⅔ cup)

2 tablespoons chopped fresh flat-leaf parsley

¼ cup honey

2 tablespoons freshly squeezed orange juice

¼ teaspoon freshly ground black pepper

⅛ teaspoon salt

Combine the fennel, onion, oranges, and parsley in a salad bowl and mix well.

For the dressing, whisk together the honey, orange juice, black pepper, and salt in a small bowl. Pour over the salad and toss to coat. Serve about ⅔ cup to each person.

Yield = 4 servings
Fat per serving = 0.26 g.
Calories per serving = 103.2

WE CAN'T THINK OF many flavor combinations that conjure up the image of Italy better than orange, fennel, and parsley. Although some American cooks confuse fennel with anise and shy away from it, fennel smells only mildly like licorice and has a sweet, mild flavor all its own. We pair it here with temple oranges, whose slight tartness provides a pleasing contrast. Both fennel, or *finocchio*, and temple oranges have the added advantage of being available in the produce-scarce winter months.

Roasted Eggplant and Fennel Salad

1 pound purple eggplant (about 1 small eggplant)

2 teaspoons coarse salt

8 ounces *cipolline*

1 pound fennel (about 1 large bulb)

6 ounces red bell pepper (about 1 pepper), halved, cored, and seeded

4 large cloves garlic

Olive oil cooking spray

1/4 cup light corn syrup

1/4 cup white wine vinegar

1 tablespoon plus 1 teaspoon chopped fresh oregano

4 cups watercress

Trim and quarter the eggplant lengthwise, then cut each long piece crosswise into 1/2-inch-thick triangles. Place in a colander, sprinkle with the salt, and set in the sink to drain for 15 minutes.

Meanwhile, blanch the *cipolline* in boiling water for 30 seconds. As soon as they have cooled enough to handle, slip off their outer skins.

Preheat the oven to 400 degrees.

Trim and quarter the fennel bulb lengthwise, then cut the quarters into 1/4-inch slices. Place in a microwave-safe container, cover with plastic wrap, and microwave at full strength for about 1 minute, until the fennel just begins to feel warm to the touch. (You can also blanch the fennel in lightly salted boiling water for about 2 minutes.)

Pat the eggplant pieces dry with paper towels. Arrange the eggplant, *cipolline*, fennel, bell pepper, and garlic in a single layer on a baking sheet. Spray the vegetables lightly with olive oil and toss to coat. Roast for 15 minutes, toss again, and roast for about 15 minutes more, until the eggplant is soft.

Transfer the eggplant, *cipolline*, and fennel, to a mixing bowl. Peel the bell pepper, cut it into strips, and add it to the mixture in the bowl.

For the dressing, combine the corn syrup, vinegar, and oregano in a small bowl. Mash in the roasted garlic and whisk until smoothly blended. Pour the dressing over the vegetables and toss to coat.

On each of 4 salad plates, mound ¾ cup of the vegetable mixture over 1 cup of the watercress.

Yield = 4 servings
Fat per serving = 0.50 g.
Calories per serving = 132.3

Bean and Tomato Salad

We have long used Great Northern beans, never knowing of their Italian connection. Then we read *Red, White, and Greens,* in which Faith Willinger reports that on checking the fine print on a bag of *toscanelli,* the little Tuscan beans, in a specialty store in Florence, she learned they were really Great Northerns imported from the United States! The beans have a delicate flavor that complements other ingredients without overwhelming them. Since they are minimally cooked in this simple preparation, the canned variety really isn't a desirable alternative.

1½ cups cooked Great Northern beans (see Pantry)
8 ounces tomato (about 1 tomato), peeled, seeded, and diced (about 1 cup)
2 cloves garlic, minced
1 tablespoon fresh thyme leaves
Salt and freshly ground black pepper to taste

In a medium nonstick skillet, combine the beans, tomato, garlic, and thyme. Stir to combine. Cook over medium heat for about 10 minutes, stirring occasionally, to heat through. Add salt and pepper to taste.

Remove from the heat and cool to room temperature before serving.

Serve a scant ⅔ cup to each person.

Yield = 4 servings
Fat per serving = 0.31 g.
Calories per serving = 89.5

Tuscan Bread Salad

½ cup freshly squeezed orange juice

¼ cup balsamic vinegar

¼ teaspoon freshly ground black pepper

¼ teaspoon salt

2 cloves garlic

8 ounces Italian bread (about ½ loaf), cut into ½-inch cubes (about 6 cups)

12 ounces tomatoes (about 2 tomatoes), diced (about 1¾ cups)

4 ounces Vidalia onion (about 1 small onion), chopped (about ¾ cup)

3 tablespoons shredded fresh basil

2 ounces arugula, shredded (about 1 cup, packed)

Preheat the oven to 400 degrees.

For the dressing, combine the orange juice, vinegar, black pepper, and salt in a small bowl. Press in the garlic. Whisk until smoothly blended.

Place the bread cubes on a baking sheet and toast in the oven until golden, about 10 minutes, tossing after 5 minutes.

In a salad bowl, combine the toasted bread, tomatoes, onion, basil, and arugula. Pour the dressing over and toss to coat. Cover with plastic wrap and set aside for 30 minutes. Toss, cover again, and set aside for 30 minutes more to allow the flavors to meld.

Yield = 4 servings
Fat per serving = 0.62 g.
Calories per serving = 139.6

WE TOAST THE croutons for this simple, refreshing *panzanella* after cutting the bread, so that they become crisp all over and hold their shape better once the salad is dressed. Use croutons made from Rustic Italian Bread (page 63) or a purchased loaf. The bread is tossed with the traditional tomato, onion, and basil mixture, to which we add flavorful arugula for bulk without fat or carbohydrates. The oil that would typically go into the dressing is replaced in this recipe with orange juice, joined here by balsamic vinegar.

Orzo Salad with Capers and Tomatoes

Although *orzo* means "barley" in Italian, we know orzo as a pasta that comes in the shape of little kernels of rice. Here we add tomatoes, green pepper, onions, and capers and toss the salad in a pesto-like basil, garlic, and Parmesan dressing. When you add the orzo cooking liquid to the basil mixture, it actually cooks it a bit and helps brighten the basil, rather than darkening it as oil darkens the typical pesto.

8 cups water
1⅓ cups orzo
1 clove garlic, chopped
¼ cup chopped fresh basil
1 tablespoon freshly grated Parmigiano-Reggiano cheese
2 tablespoons freshly squeezed lemon juice

8 cherry tomatoes, quartered
¼ cup chopped green bell pepper
8 large pickled cocktail onions, quartered
2 teaspoons small capers (nonpareils), drained
Salt and freshly ground black pepper to taste

Bring the water to a boil in a medium saucepan over high heat. Add the orzo and cook for 7 minutes, until tender but still firm. Drain the orzo well and transfer it to a serving bowl, reserving 2 tablespoons of the cooking liquid.

Combine the garlic, basil, Parmesan, lemon juice, and reserved cooking liquid in a food processor and process until smooth. Add the mixture to the orzo, along with the tomatoes, bell pepper, onions, capers, salt, and black pepper. Mix well.

Yield = 6 servings
Fat per serving = 0.84 g.
Calories per serving = 151.2

Roasted Pear and Frisée Salad

12 ounces Bosc pears (about 2 pears), halved and cored

3 tablespoons honey

1 tablespoon Dijon mustard

3 tablespoons white wine vinegar

4 ounces frisée, cut into bite-size pieces (about 3 cups)

2 ounces skim-milk feta cheese, crumbled (about ½ cup)

Preheat the oven to 400 degrees.

Place the pear halves in a small ovenproof dish and bake for 10 minutes.

Meanwhile, for the dressing, combine the honey and mustard in a small bowl and whisk in the vinegar.

On each of 4 salad plates, arrange ¾ cup frisée. Slice and fan a pear half over each, sprinkle with 2 tablespoons of the feta, and drizzle with 1½ tablespoons of the dressing.

Yield = 4 servings
Fat per serving = 0.90 g.
Calories per serving = 117.6

SUCCULENT ROASTED pears and tangy feta cheese top lacy frisée, a variety of curly endive, in this sophisticated salad. Select firm Bosc pairs, which hold their shape well in the oven. Remove their little seed cores with a melon baller or the tip of a spoon. Because of its assertive flavor and firm texture, we choose to use a nonfat variety of feta, a Greek cheese that our local Italian specialty market has been stocking of late.

Pizza, Focaccia, and Calzones

(Pizze, Focacce, e Calzoni)

Pizza Dough ⟿ Individual Roasted Pepper and Portobello Pizzas ⟿ Eggplant Pizza ⟿ Sun-Dried Tomato Focaccia ⟿ Focaccia Dough ⟿ Vidalia Onion and Poppy Seed Focaccia ⟿ Tomato-Basil Focaccia with Bacon ⟿ Calzone Dough ⟿ Sausage Calzones ⟿ Spinach Calzones

14. Pizza, Focaccia, and Calzones

(Pizze, Focacce, e Calzoni)

What for years passed for pizza in America—years during which, we might add, the dish was virtually unknown in most of Italy outside Naples—was all too often far too much of a good thing. On most pizzeria offerings, an excessive amount of cheese fought with layers of sausage even before the inevitable glut of optional add-ons, all piled high on a soggy crust ready to collapse under the accumulated burden. It was a bit gastronomically disconcerting to many and a nightmare to anyone attempting to limit fat intake. Today, we are glad to say, Americans have somewhat more refined options, and pizza is enjoyed throughout Italy and indeed much of the world.

Although the terms describing various members of the pizza family are somewhat imprecisely interpreted in different locations, we refer here to fairly generously topped pies with crisp crusts as pizzas, to lightly topped rectangular flatbreads with thicker, chewier crusts as focacce, and to stuffed pockets made with pizza-like dough as calzones.

Because Italian pizzas have always been more restrained than their early American imitators, leaning more toward the use of vegetables and herbs than toward "double cheese and pepperoni," little has to be done in the way of adaptation for the fat-free kitchen except to limit the use of olive oil.

Our sampling includes an eggplant and tomato pizza, a pizza featuring sliced portobello mushrooms scattered over a red pepper puree, a focaccia with bits of bacon in the crust and a topping of tomato and basil, and a nutty-tasting focaccia topped with sweet onions and poppy seeds. Calzones are served up stuffed with robustly seasoned turkey sausage and with a spinach-and-ricotta-cheese mixture.

Pizza Dough

⅓ cup lukewarm water (105 to 115 degrees on an instant-read thermometer)

¾ teaspoon sugar

1 packet (¼ ounce) active dry yeast

2¾ cups unbleached all-purpose flour

½ cup semolina flour

1 teaspoon salt

¾ cup plus 3 tablespoons room-temperature water

Olive oil cooking spray

In a small bowl, whisk together the lukewarm water and the sugar. Whisk in the yeast and set aside for about 5 minutes, until the mixture is bubbly.

In the bowl of a food processor, combine the flours and salt. Process for about 30 seconds to mix. Scrape in the yeast mixture. With the machine running, drizzle the room-temperature water through the feed tube to form a dough ball. Turn the machine off and feel the dough; if it is very dry at this stage, turn the machine back on and add an additional tablespoon of room-temperature water. Process for 1 minute more.

Remove the dough to a ceramic or glass bowl that has been lightly coated with olive oil spray and cover tightly with plastic wrap. Set aside for about 1½ hours, until the dough doubles in size.

This dough can be prepared up to 3 days in advance, sealed in an airtight plastic bag, and stored in the refrigerator.

Yield = Enough dough for 8 individual 4-inch round pizzas, two 10-inch round pizzas, or one 12¼-by-17-inch sheet pizza

Individual Roasted Pepper and Portobello Pizzas

1 pound leeks (2 to 3 leeks), cleaned, trimmed, and thinly sliced (about 4 cups)

¼ cup dry white wine

7 ounces roasted sweet red pepper (see Pantry)

1 tablespoon capers, drained

1 large clove garlic, peeled

1 tablespoon plus 2 teaspoons chopped fresh oregano

Thirty-two ¼-inch-thick slices portobello mushrooms (about 8 ounces)

1 recipe Pizza Dough (page 214)

1 tablespoon plus 1 teaspoon freshly grated Parmigiano-Reggiano cheese

Preheat the oven to 450 degrees. Heat a medium nonstick skillet over medium-high heat. Add the leeks and cook 1 minute; then, stirring constantly, cook another 30 seconds. Add the wine and continue to cook, stirring occasionally, until the wine has evaporated and the leeks are dry, about 3½ minutes more. Remove from the heat and set aside.

In a food processor, combine the roasted pepper, capers, garlic, and 1 teaspoon of the oregano. Process to a smooth puree.

Arrange the mushrooms on a nonstick baking sheet and bake for 8 minutes.

Meanwhile, divide the dough into 8 pieces and form each into a 4-inch circle. Place the dough circles on a large nonstick baking sheet. Jab them all over with the tines of a fork and bake for about 5 minutes, until they are just beginning to color; if puffy, poke some more holes in the dough.

Spread 1 tablespoon of the pepper puree over each pizza. Top each with ¼ cup leeks, 4 portobello slices, ½ teaspoon of the remaining oregano, and ½ teaspoon Parmesan cheese. Bake for 10 to 11 minutes, until golden.

Yield = 8 individual pizzas
Fat per pizza = 0.84 g.
Calories per pizza = 204.4

THESE ELEGANT individual vegetarian pizzas feature bits of meaty portobello mushrooms scattered atop a roasted red pepper puree—minutes in the making if you start with preroasted peppers—which replaces the typical tomato sauce. For variety, use 8 ounces medium shrimp (about 32 shrimp), shelled, deveined, and cut in half lengthwise, instead of the mushrooms. In the Italian fashion, skip the Parmesan garnish if you top your pizzas with seafood.

Eggplant Pizza

THIS PIZZA IS DOTTED with bits of eggplant as well as fresh plum tomatoes, oven-roasted just enough to boost their flavor and dry them out a bit. In the days when these ingredients first made their way to Italy (eggplant from India and tomatoes from the Americas), the combination would have been considered doubly dangerous, since both are members of the infamous nightshade family and consuming them was thought to cause madness. Now the combination offers a healthful alternative to the high-fat pizza toppings usually consumed in the United States.

We partially bake the dough before topping, to seal the crust and keep it crisp. Instead of making two 10-inch round pizzas, you could make 1 large rectangular pizza, spreading the dough to cover a 12¼-by-17-inch baking pan.

¾ pound purple eggplant (about 1 small eggplant), cut into ½-inch cubes

2¾ teaspoons coarse salt

1 pound plum tomatoes (4 to 5 tomatoes), cut into ¼-inch rounds

Olive oil cooking spray

2 tablespoons chopped fresh basil leaves

½ cup skim-milk ricotta cheese

1 recipe Pizza Dough (page 214)

2 tablespoons minced roasted garlic (see Pantry)

2 tablespoons chopped fresh flat-leaf parsley

1 tablespoon freshly grated Parmigiano-Reggiano cheese

¼ teaspoon freshly ground black pepper

Place the eggplant in a colander and sprinkle it with 2 teaspoons of the salt. Toss and allow the eggplant to drain in the sink for 30 minutes.

Preheat the oven to 350 degrees.

Toss the eggplant again and let drain for 30 minutes more. Meanwhile, fit a baking sheet with a rack and place the tomato rounds on the rack. Sprinkle with the remaining ¾ teaspoon salt. Bake for about 30 minutes, until the tomatoes are starting to dry on top. Turn the rounds over and bake for 30 minutes more.

While the tomatoes are baking on the second side, rinse the eggplant under cold running water for about 1 minute, then wrap the cubes in a clean towel and squeeze out the excess moisture. Spray a baking sheet to coat with olive oil. Arrange the eggplant on the sheet and bake for 15 minutes. Toss and bake for about 15 minutes more, until just beginning to brown.

When both the tomatoes and the eggplant are done, remove them from the oven and turn the oven up to 450 degrees.

In a small bowl, combine the basil and ricotta cheese.

Cut the dough in half and form each half into a 10-inch circle. Place the circles on pizza pans or nonstick baking sheets. Jab them all over with the tines of a fork. Bake for 5 minutes; if puffy, poke some more.

Spread 1 tablespoon of the roasted garlic over the crust of each pizza. Layer each with half the ricotta mixture, half the eggplant, and half the tomatoes. Sprinkle 1 tablespoon of the parsley over each pizza, and top with ½ tablespoon of the Parmesan cheese and ⅛ teaspoon of the black pepper. Return to the oven and bake for about 10 minutes more, until golden.

Cut each pizza into 8 pieces and serve two slices per person.

Yield = 8 servings
Fat per serving = 0.85 g.
Calories per serving = 205.9

Sun-Dried Tomato Focaccia

THIS FOCACCIA, WHICH is a bit denser than the average one, has an intense flavor derived from substituting the reconstituting liquid from the sun-dried tomatoes for water when you make the dough.

To "sun-dry" your own tomatoes indoors, cut plum tomatoes in half lengthwise and bake them in a 170-degree oven, cut side up, for about 6 hours, until they are moisture-free but still pliable, or dry them in a dehydrator according to the manufacturer's directions. For this recipe, we prefer the robust flavor of red tomatoes to that of the milder yellow variety.

8 sun-dried red tomato halves
1 1/4 cups cold water
1 tablespoon honey
1/4 cup lukewarm water (105 to 115 degrees on an instant-read thermometer)
1 packet (1/4 ounce) active dry yeast
2 3/4 cups unbleached all-purpose flour
1/2 cup whole wheat pastry flour
1 tablespoon salt
1 large egg white, plus 1 additional egg white beaten with 1 tablespoon water
Olive oil cooking spray
1/2 tablespoon coarse salt

Combine the sun-dried tomatoes and 1/2 cup of the cold water in a small microwave-safe bowl. Cover with plastic wrap and microwave at full power for about 1 minute to reconstitute the tomatoes. (You can also reconstitute the tomatoes by combining them with enough boiling water to cover and letting them steep until soft, 20 to 30 minutes.) Remove the tomatoes and squeeze out the excess moisture. Transfer the liquid to a measuring cup, add just enough of the remaining 3/4 cup cold water to make 1 cup, and reserve. Chop the tomatoes. (You should have about 1/4 cup.)

In a small bowl, whisk together the honey and lukewarm water. Whisk in the yeast and set aside for about 10 minutes, until bubbly.

In a food processor, combine the all-purpose flour, whole wheat pastry flour, salt, and 1 egg white. Process for 1 minute, then scrape in the yeast mixture and add the sun-dried tomatoes. Turn the machine on and drizzle in the reserved tomato water through the feed tube. Once a dough ball forms, process for about 1 minute more. Transfer the dough ball to a large ceramic or glass bowl lightly coated with olive oil spray. Roll the ball to coat. Cover the bowl with a clean, dry dish towel and set the dough aside for about 1 hour, until it has doubled in size and no longer springs back to the touch.

Remove the dough to a 9 1/4-by-13 1/4-inch baking sheet that has been lightly coated with olive oil spray. Push the dough out over the surface of the sheet to cover it evenly. Cover it with the towel and set aside for 15 minutes.

With your hands, push the dough flat, leaving only a $\frac{1}{2}$-inch raised outer border. Paint the dough with the egg-white-and-water mixture and sprinkle it with the coarse salt. Cover it again and set aside for 15 minutes more.

Meanwhile, preheat the oven to 350 degrees.

Bake the focaccia for about 45 minutes, until the top is lightly browned and the crust sounds hollow when tapped. Transfer the baking sheet to a wire rack to cool. Cut into 12 squares about 3-by-$3\frac{1}{4}$ inches. Serve warm or at room temperature.

Yield = 12 servings
Fat per serving = 0.38 g.
Calories per serving = 116.6

Focaccia Dough

⅓ cup lukewarm water (105 to 115 degrees on an instant-read thermometer)
1 packet (¼ ounce) active dry yeast
1¼ teaspoons sugar
½ teaspoon salt

¾ cup skim milk, at room temperature
2½ cups plus 2 tablespoons bread flour
Olive oil cooking spray

Put the lukewarm water in a small bowl. Add the yeast and sugar and whisk until dissolved. Set aside for about 5 minutes, until bubbly.

Meanwhile, dissolve the salt in the skim milk in a mixing bowl. Slowly stir in 1½ cups of the flour with a wooden spoon. Stir in the yeast mixture. In increments, stir in 1 cup more of the flour. If the flour is not being fully incorporated, knead it into the dough by hand.

Sprinkle the remaining 2 tablespoons flour over a work surface. Turn the dough out onto the surface and knead in the flour. Continue to knead for about 5 minutes, until the dough feels smooth and elastic.

Transfer the dough to a ceramic or glass bowl that has been coated lightly with the olive oil spray. Cover the bowl with plastic wrap and set the dough aside at room temperature for about 1½ hours, until doubled in size.

Yield = Enough dough for 1 thin 11-by-15-inch focaccia or 1 thick 9¼-by-13¼-inch focaccia

Vidalia Onion and Poppy Seed Focaccia

8 ounces Vidalia onions (about 2 small onions), peeled, halved lengthwise, then thinly sliced crosswise (about 2 cups)

1/3 cup water

1/2 teaspoon cornstarch

Olive oil cooking spray

1 recipe Focaccia Dough (page 220)

3/4 teaspoon coarse salt

1/4 teaspoon poppy seeds

Preheat the oven to 425 degrees. Line a baking dish with aluminum foil.

Place the onions in the baking dish. Bake for 5 minutes, stirring after 2½ minutes. Remove, leaving the oven turned on.

Combine the water and cornstarch in a small bowl and mix thoroughly.

Spray a 15-by-11-inch baking pan lightly with olive oil. Work the dough to cover the entire pan evenly, pushing it into the corners. Using the bottom of a wooden spoon handle, make little indentations all over the surface of the dough. Paint the dough with the water-and-cornstarch wash. Scatter the onions over the dough, then the salt and the poppy seeds.

Cover loosely with plastic wrap and let sit for 45 minutes.

Bake the focaccia for about 25 minutes, until it has browned and the edges are very crisp.

Remove from the oven and cool for at least 5 minutes. Cut into fifteen 3-by-3½-inch pieces. Serve immediately.

Yield = 15 servings
Fat per serving = 0.26 g.
Calories per serving = 79.8

ALTHOUGH *FOCACCE* are Genoese in origin, this delicate, thin rendition is finished with a particularly American flourish— wonderfully sweet Vidalia onions. We employ an old pizza baker's trick of prebaking the onions a bit before topping the pizza, which boosts their natural sweetness, as does the sprinkle of nutty poppy seeds.

Tomato-Basil Focaccia with Bacon

FOCACCE VARY according to local whim, sporting a mix of seasonal ingredients. Some are even sweetened with sugar or made with egg in the dough. We knead a generous supply of turkey bacon into the slightly puffy crust of this focaccia, our healthful take on a regional variation made with pork cracklings. Baking the bacon produces crisper strips than frying or cooking it in a microwave oven. Use our proportions for both the bacon and the basil as a departure point, adding a bit more of either to taste.

6 slices turkey bacon
1 recipe Focaccia Dough (page 220)
Olive oil cooking spray
$\frac{1}{3}$ cup water
2 teaspoons cornstarch

4 ounces very ripe tomato (about 1 small tomato), seeded and chopped (about $\frac{1}{2}$ cup)
2 tablespoons chopped fresh basil

Preheat the oven to 425 degrees. Line a baking dish with aluminum foil.

Put the bacon in the prepared dish and bake for about 12 minutes, until crisp. Remove the bacon to cool and leave the oven on. When the bacon has cooled enough to handle, chop it. (You should have a little less than $\frac{1}{2}$ cup.)

Turn the dough out onto a work surface and knead the bacon into it.

Spray a $9\frac{1}{4}$-by-$13\frac{1}{4}$-inch baking pan once with the olive oil. Place the dough in the pan and press it evenly over the surface, taking care to work it into the corners. Dimple the dough by making small indentations all over the surface with the end of a wooden spoon handle.

Combine the water and cornstarch in a small bowl, mix well, and paint the dough with the wash. Scatter the tomatoes and basil over the dough, cover it loosely with plastic wrap, and set it aside for 30 minutes.

Bake the focaccia for 15 to 18 minutes, until golden and puffy. Cut it into twelve 3-by-$3\frac{1}{4}$-inch servings. Serve warm.

Yield = 12 servings
Fat per serving = 0.73 g.
Calories per serving = 114.9

Calzone Dough

¼ cup lukewarm water (105 to 115 degrees on an instant-read thermometer)
1 tablespoon sugar
1 packet (¼ ounce) active dry yeast
3½ cups unbleached all-purpose flour

¼ cup whole wheat flour
½ tablespoon coarse salt
2 large egg whites
1 cup skim milk
Olive oil cooking spray

Combine the water and sugar in a small bowl. Stir in the yeast and set aside for about 5 minutes, until bubbly.

Combine the flours and salt in the bowl of a food processor. Process for 1 minute to mix thoroughly. Scrape in the yeast mixture. Turn the machine on and drizzle the egg whites through the feed tube. Drizzle in the skim milk until a dough ball forms. (You may not need to use the whole 1 cup.) Continue to process for another full minute.

Transfer the dough to a ceramic or glass bowl lightly coated with the olive oil spray, cover the bowl tightly with plastic wrap, and set the dough aside to double in size, about 2 hours.

Yield = Enough dough for 6 to 8 calzones

CALZONES ARE another Neapolitan invention whose popularity has now spread far and wide. This dough yields turnover-like pastries that are considerably thinner and lighter and slightly crisper than the unfortunate imitations sold as fast food in the United States. Use the dough to make Sausage Calzones (page 224) and Spinach Calzones (page 226).

Sausage Calzones

We think of this as our Italianized version of sausage en croûte. The homemade sausage, made in the food processor from lean turkey, has a fennel, thyme, and oregano seasoning that lends a flavor similar to that of fattier pork sausages.

Olive oil cooking spray

1/2 pound turkey breast tenderloin, cut into chunks

3/4 teaspoon fennel seeds

2 teaspoons dried thyme

1/2 teaspoon dried oregano

1/4 teaspoon paprika

1/8 teaspoon freshly ground black pepper

1/4 teaspoon crushed red pepper flakes

3/4 teaspoon salt

2 cloves garlic, peeled

8 ounces green bell pepper (about 1 pepper), cored, seeded, and chopped (about 1 cup)

6 ounces purple (red) onion (about 1 small onion), diced (about 1 cup)

1/2 cup chopped tomatoes

1/4 cup chopped fresh flat-leaf parsley

1/2 teaspoon freshly grated Parmigiano-Reggiano cheese

1 recipe Calzone Dough (page 223)

1 large egg white mixed with 1 tablespoon water

Preheat the oven to 400 degrees. Coat a baking sheet with the olive oil spray.

Combine the turkey, fennel seed, thyme, oregano, paprika, black pepper, crushed red pepper, and 1/2 teaspoon of the salt in a bowl and mix to coat the turkey. Transfer the mixture to a food processor, add the garlic, and process to a fine chop. (You should have about 1 cup of sausage meat.)

Combine the sausage, bell pepper, and onion in a medium nonstick skillet. Stirring occasionally, cook the mixture over medium heat until the meat is well browned, 3 to 4 minutes. Remove it to a bowl and mix in the tomatoes, parsley, Parmesan cheese, and the remaining 1/4 teaspoon salt.

Cut the dough into 8 equal pieces and form each piece into a 6-inch circle about 1/4-inch thick. Put about 6 tablespoons of the sausage mixture on one half of each circle and paint the outer borders with the egg-and-water wash. Fold the dough over the filling and crimp the edges together with a fork. Paint the top of the dough with the wash. Prick each calzone three times with the tines of a fork.

Place the calzones on the prepared sheet and bake for about 23 minutes, until golden. Remove from the oven and let cool for about 10 minutes before serving.

Yield = 8 calzones
Fat per calzone = 1.00 g.
Calories per calzone = 254.0

Spinach Calzones

CALZONE TRANSLATES as "trouser leg," probably a reference to the sausage shape in which calzones were made before they evolved into the half-moons we know today. The spinach and ricotta cheese filling in these tasty little crescents is accented by a bit of chopped sun-dried tomato and some nutmeg. Use fresh nutmeg if at all possible; it's quite a bit more robust and aromatic than the commercial variety.

Olive oil cooking spray
1 ounce sun-dried tomatoes (8 to 10)
$1/4$ cup hot water
2 tablespoons chopped fresh basil
2 tablespoons chopped fresh flat-leaf parsley
2 ounces scallions (about 2 scallions), trimmed and chopped (about $1/4$ cup)
One 10-ounce box frozen chopped spinach, thawed and squeezed dry
$3/4$ cup skim-milk ricotta cheese
$1/4$ cup nonfat liquid egg substitute
$1/4$ teaspoon freshly ground black pepper
$1/4$ teaspoon grated nutmeg
1 teaspoon salt
$1/2$ teaspoon freshly grated Parmigiano-Reggiano cheese
1 recipe Calzone Dough (page 223)
1 large egg white mixed with 1 tablespoon water

Preheat the oven to 400 degrees. Coat a baking sheet with olive oil spray.

In a small bowl, combine the sun-dried tomatoes and the hot water. Set aside for about 20 to 30 minutes to allow the tomatoes to reconstitute. Drain and chop the tomatoes (you should have about 2 tablespoons).

In a large bowl, combine the tomatoes, basil, parsley, scallions, spinach, ricotta cheese, egg substitute, black pepper, nutmeg, salt, and Parmesan cheese.

Cut the dough into 6 equal pieces and form each piece into a 7-inch circle about $1/4$-inch thick. Put about $1/3$ cup of the filling mixture on one half of each dough circle and paint the outer borders with the egg-and-water wash. Fold the dough over the filling and crimp the edges together with a fork. Paint the top of the dough with the wash. Prick each calzone twice with the tines of a fork.

Place the calzones on the prepared baking sheet. Bake for about 23 minutes, until golden. Remove from the oven and let cool for about 10 minutes before serving.

Yield = 6 calzones
Fat per calzone = 0.99 g.
Calories per calzone = 314.0

Desserts

(Dolci)

Roasted Pears and Blueberries in Balsamic Vinegar ⟶ Campari Sorbet ⟶ Green Apple Granita ⟶ Lemon Gelato ⟶ Amaretto Semifreddo ⟶ Chocolate Tiramisù ⟶ Panettone Bread Pudding ⟶ Chocolate-Cherry Rice Pudding ⟶ Pear and Honey Risotto ⟶ Apple Cake ⟶ Torta di Ricotta ⟶ Jennie's Easter Wheat Pie ⟶ Anise Biscotti ⟶ Chocolate Raisin Biscotti

15. Desserts

(Dolci)

The desserts eaten in Italian homes tend to be simple and straightforward—fruit foremost, lots of it and always in season, frozen desserts, homey puddings, and maybe now and then a special-occasion cake or tart. As these are mostly healthful indulgences to begin with, the main adjustments to be made in the fat-free kitchen are a matter of replacing high-fat dairy products with skim milk and egg-white-based products.

Our sampling begins, appropriately, with mixed macerated fruit, uniquely combined here with basil leaves and sprinkled with balsamic vinegar. We progress through a medley of frozen desserts, including Campari Sorbet, Green Apple Granita, Lemon Gelato, and Amaretto Semifreddo. Puddings include fat-free renditions of two favorite but usually high-fat treats, a tiramisù and a novel bread pudding made from panettone, as well as a chocolaty rice pudding and a sweet risotto.

We include as well a simple fruit-filled cake, an airy ricotta cheesecake, and a traditional Easter wheat pie. Last, perhaps as appropriate for daytime snacks as for dessert, is a choice of biscotti, one crisp, savory, and very sophisticated, the other softer, sweeter, and more comforting in nature.

MACERATED FRUIT IS
an Italian favorite, though
the fruit usually steeps in
wine. We love the tart tang
lent by sweet balsamic
vinegar, accented with
aromatic fresh basil.
Roasting the pears first is a
quick and easy step that
adds immensely to the flavor
and texture of the finished
dessert.

Roasted Pears and Blueberries in Balsamic Vinegar

1 pound Bosc pears (about 2 large
    pears), peeled, halved, and cored
1/2 pint blueberries (about 1 cup)

2 tablespoons balsamic vinegar
1 teaspoon thinly sliced basil

Preheat the oven to 400 degrees.

Place the pear halves in a small ovenproof dish and bake until they are browned and tender, about 10 minutes. Cool, then cut them into 1/2-inch cubes.

In a bowl, combine the pears, blueberries, vinegar, and basil. Toss to mix, cover with plastic wrap, and refrigerate for 1 hour.

Yield = 6 servings
Fat per serving = 0.41 g.
Calories per serving = 60.0

Campari Sorbet

1 cup water

1 cup sugar

½ teaspoon grated orange zest

2 cups freshly squeezed orange juice

1 cup Campari

Combine the water and sugar in a small saucepan. Bring to a boil over high heat and boil for 5 minutes. Remove the mixture to a glass container and allow it to cool to room temperature. Cover and place it in the freezer for about 1 hour to chill through.

Stir in the orange zest, orange juice, and Campari. Transfer the sorbet to a 1-quart ice cream maker and freeze according to the manufacturer's directions.

Yield = 8 servings
Fat per serving = 0.1 g.
Calories per serving = 155.3

CAMPARI, THE vibrant red beverage from Milan, is the basis of the Negroni cocktail you may sip before dinner and the primary flavoring in this distinctive sorbet. It's very refreshing and would work equally well as a palate cleanser or a dessert. This sorbet takes a bit longer to freeze than most because of the alcohol in the Campari. We usually make it a day in advance, transfer it to a container with a tight-fitting lid and store it in the freezer to firm up.

Green Apple Granita

BARRY'S FIRST exposure to a green apple ice was in the form of a sorbet, savored during a rainy New Year's Day supper some 10 years ago at a little bistro in Paris with our friend Claudia and her daughter. It was so good that the three of them still rave about it, and Barry has been busily trying out his own renditions ever since. This granita, a bit coarser than the sorbet on which it is modeled, is a pretty green-beige, its color lent by European sparkling cider made from green apples. The addition of a little honey thickens the mixture and smooths the ice a bit.

1 tablespoon honey
1 cup sugar
1 cup water
2 large Granny Smith apples (about 21 ounces total), peeled, cored, and cut into chunks (about 4 cups)

2 tablespoons freshly squeezed lemon juice
1 cup imported sparkling cider
2 tablespoons vodka

In a small saucepan, combine the honey, sugar, and water. Bring the mixture to a boil over medium heat and boil for about 10 minutes, until reduced to 1 cup.

Transfer the syrup to the bowl of a food processor. Add the apple chunks and the lemon juice and process to a smooth puree. Remove the puree to a bowl and stir in the cider and vodka. Cover and chill in the freezer for about 1 hour, then transfer to an ice cream maker and finish according to the manufacturer's directions.

Yield = 8 servings
Fat per serving = 0.25 g.
Calories per serving = 169.8

Lemon Gelato

1 tablespoon finely grated lemon zest

⅓ cup freshly squeezed lemon juice, strained

⅔ cup sugar

½ cup nonfat liquid egg substitute

1⅓ cups evaporated skim milk

1 teaspoon vanilla extract

In a medium saucepan, whisk together the lemon zest, lemon juice, sugar, and egg substitute. Whisking constantly, cook over medium heat for 12 to 15 minutes, until the mixture registers 170 degrees on an instant-read thermometer; take care not to let it boil. Pour it through a fine-mesh strainer into a medium mixing bowl. Stir in the evaporated milk and vanilla.

Cover with plastic wrap and refrigerate for at least 2 hours, then transfer to an ice cream maker and freeze according to the manufacturer's directions.

Yield = 8 servings
Fat per serving = 0.02 g.
Calories per serving = 82.3

ALTHOUGH IT TASTES more like a rich French ice cream, this gelato is actually as low in fat as the typical ice milk sold by *gelaterie* throughout Italy, in this case as a result of our using egg substitute made from egg whites. If you love ice cream as much as the Italians do (and we do) you can enjoy this cool indulgence with guiltless abandon!

Amaretto Semifreddo

SEMIFREDDO WHICH means "partially frozen," is the name given to a mousse or custard that is frozen but not whipped in an ice cream maker. This heavenly semifreddo derives its nutty flavor from amaretti, the "little bitter" almond cookies you often find wrapped in squares of brightly colored paper, and a bit of amaretto liqueur, homemade (page 257) or store-bought. For the best results, chill a loaf pan or soufflé dish in the freezer while you prepare the mixture.

1 tablespoon plus 2½ cups water
1 teaspoon unflavored gelatin
1 cup evaporated skim milk, chilled
2 tablespoons amaretto liqueur
¼ cup nonfat liquid egg substitute

1 large egg white
3 tablespoons sugar
6 amaretti, roughly crumbled (about
 ⅓ cup crumbs)

Place a metal mixing bowl and the beaters from an electric mixer in the freezer until well chilled.

Put 1 tablespoon of the water in a small bowl and sprinkle the gelatin on top. Set aside for 5 minutes. Microwave at full power for 20 seconds to liquefy, then stir to dissolve the gelatin completely. (You can also liquefy and dissolve the gelatin by sprinkling it over ¼ cup water in a small saucepan, letting stand for 1 minute, and stirring over low heat.) Allow the mixture to cool for 7 to 8 minutes, until it is no longer warm but still liquid.

Meanwhile, bring the remaining 2½ cups water to a simmer in a medium saucepan.

Pour the evaporated milk into the chilled mixing bowl. Fit an electric mixer with the chilled beaters and beat the milk at high speed for a few minutes, until stiff peaks form. Add the amaretto and the gelatin mixture and continue to beat for about 1 minute to bring it back to stiff peaks.

Combine the egg substitute, egg white, and sugar in a heatproof glass bowl just big enough to sit over, not in, the water in the saucepan. Whisk lightly and place the bowl over the simmering water. Whisking vigorously, heat for 5 to 6 minutes, until the mixture registers 140 degrees on an instant-read thermometer and is thick enough to coat the back of a spoon.

Remove the bowl to a towel-lined work surface and whisk until steam is no longer emanating from the mixture, about 3 minutes. Stir in the crumbled amaretti with a wooden spoon. Fold the mixture into the whipped evaporated milk.

Transfer the semifreddo to the chilled loaf pan or soufflé dish, cover with plastic wrap, and freeze for at least 8 hours.

Yield = 8 servings
Fat per serving = 0.44 g.
Calories per serving = 89.9

Chocolate Tiramisù

1 tablespoon unsweetened Dutch
  processed cocoa powder
1 teaspoon light corn syrup
2 teaspoons hot water
1 teaspoon Marsala wine
4 teaspoons Grand Marnier liqueur

6 crisp Italian ladyfingers
$^1\!/_4$ cup strong brewed coffee
$^1\!/_4$ cup nonfat liquid egg substitute
2 tablespoons confectioners' sugar
$^2\!/_3$ cup Mascarpone (page 24)

In a small bowl, whisk the cocoa powder, corn syrup, and hot water together until smooth. Mix in the Marsala and 2 teaspoons of the Grand Marnier. Set aside.

Break the ladyfingers in half and place them on a plate. Drizzle them with the coffee and the remaining 2 teaspoons Grand Marnier.

In a mixing bowl, combine the egg substitute and confectioners' sugar. Whisk until light and foamy. Whisk in the cocoa powder mixture, then fold in the Mascarpone. (You should have about 1 cup of the filling.)

Place half a ladyfinger on the bottom of each of four wide-mouthed champagne glasses. Layer about 8 teaspoons of the filling over the ladyfinger in each glass, then 2 more ladyfinger halves, and finally about 8 more teaspoons of filling. Cover the boats with plastic wrap and chill for 2 to 3 hours before serving.

Yield = 4 servings
Fat per serving = 0.62 g.
Calories per serving = 113.8

Panettone Bread Pudding

⅓ cup Marsala wine

3 cups evaporated skim milk

1 cup nonfat liquid egg substitute

⅓ cup light brown sugar, firmly
   packed

1 pound panettone, cut into 1-inch
   cubes (about 6 cups)

About 4 cups boiling water

Combine the Marsala, evaporated milk, egg substitute, and brown sugar in a large bowl. Whisk to combine, then stir in the bread cubes. Set aside for about 20 minutes.

Preheat the oven to 350 degrees.

Pour the bread cube mixture into a 9¼-inch nonstick loaf pan. Place the loaf pan inside a larger baking pan or baking dish set in the middle of the oven. Pour enough boiling water into the larger pan to come halfway up the sides of the loaf pan. Bake for 55 to 65 minutes, until the pudding is set in the center and no longer jiggles when shaken.

Let the pudding cool in the pan on a wire rack. Serve at room temperature or chilled.

Yield = 10 servings
Fat per serving = 0.32 g.
Calories per serving = 150.9

OLD-FASHIONED BREAD pudding is all the rage these days, but you seldom see it made with panettone, our favorite base, on either side of the Atlantic. Rich and enhanced by an intriguing dose of Marsala, this pudding is nonetheless low in fat—made with skim milk, egg-white-based egg substitute, and our own fat-free Milanese Panettone (page 72; you'll need about ½ loaf). You can use a purchased panettone in the recipe, but the final fat count will be somewhat higher.

For a dramatic presentation, divide the pudding mixture among 10 individual 4-ounce round brioche molds rather than using the single loaf pan and bake the individual puddings for only about 45 minutes.

Chocolate-Cherry Rice Pudding

If THIS SOUNDS TO you like risotto by another name, you're right. It's a chocolaty dessert risotto, studded with cherries and chilled. Chilling intensifies the dense cocoa flavor and lends an intriguing texture—quite stiff, with the grains of rice just ever so slightly chewy. Serve it using an ice cream scoop.

3 tablespoons Dutch processed cocoa powder
½ tablespoon sugar
2 tablespoons boiling water
1 tablespoon light-corn syrup

3 cups skim milk
1 cup Arborio or Carnaroli rice
½ cup dried cherries
2 tablespoons Grand Marnier liqueur

In a small bowl, combine the cocoa powder, sugar, boiling water, and corn syrup. Mix thoroughly.

In a medium saucepan over medium heat, scald the milk just until bubbles begin to appear around the edge. (Do not bring to a boil.) Reduce the heat to very low and stir in the cocoa mixture.

Preheat a large, heavy-bottomed saucepan over medium heat. Add the rice and cook for about 2 minutes, stirring constantly, until the shells look translucent. Stirring vigorously, slowly add 1 cup of the milk mixture. When the liquid has been mostly absorbed and small craters dot the surface, add another ½ cup of the milk. Stir and bring back to a simmer. When this addition has been mostly absorbed, stir in another ½ cup, then stir in the cherries. Add the remaining milk mixture ½ cup at a time, stirring after each addition; with the last, stir in the Grand Marnier. Continue to cook and stir until all the liquid has been absorbed and the rice is creamy. Preparation of this pudding should take 25 to 27 minutes from the first addition of liquid to the rice.

Transfer the pudding to a bowl or container, cover, and refrigerate for 2 hours. Scoop ¾ cup into each of 6 bowls and allow it to sit for 5 minutes before serving.

Yield = 6 servings
Fat per serving = 0.65 g.
Calories per serving = 252.8

Pear and Honey Risotto

12 ounces Bosc pears (about 2 small
    pears), peeled and cut into $1/2$- to
    $3/4$-inch cubes (about $1^1/2$ cups)
2 cups water
$1/4$ cup freshly squeezed lemon juice
3 cups skim milk
1 cup Arborio or Carnaroli rice

1 cinnamon stick
2 tablespoons Marsala wine
1 tablespoon acacia honey
$1/3$ cup golden raisins
$3/4$ teaspoon vanilla extract
1 teaspoon grated orange zest

SWEET RISOTTO IS AN unexpected treat. In this recipe it's a lovely risotto speckled with bits of pear and golden raisins and finished with a sprinkle of orange zest. The thin, pale acacia honey—the best-known is from Hungary, but it is also produced in Italy—adds flavor without unwanted color or viscosity. We like to serve this dessert stylishly in short-stemmed Gibson glasses.

Combine the pears, water, and lemon juice in a bowl and set aside.

Scald the milk in a medium saucepan over medium heat until bubbles begin to form around the edge. Reduce the heat to maintain a simmer.

Preheat a large, heavy-bottomed saucepan over medium heat. Stirring constantly, add the rice and cook for 2 minutes. While stirring vigorously, slowly add 1 cup of the milk and the cinnamon stick. When the milk has been mostly absorbed and small craters dot the surface, add another $1/2$ cup of milk. Stir and bring back to a simmer. Continue to add the remaining milk $1/2$ cup at a time, stirring after each addition. With the last addition, stir in the wine, honey, raisins, and vanilla. Drain and add the pears. Continue to cook and stir until all the liquid has been absorbed and the rice is creamy. Remove the cinnamon stick and fold in the orange zest. Preparation of this risotto should take 28 to 30 minutes from the first addition of milk.

Serve $2/3$ cup to each person, hot or at room temperature.

Yield = 6 servings
Fat per serving = 0.58 g.
Calories per serving = 238.3

Apple Cake

This cake is in many ways a quintessentially Italian dessert—simple, filled with fruit, and not too sweet or rich. It reminded an Italian-American houseguest of ours so much of the cakes his mother used to bake that he ate several slices.

The Fuji apples break up as the cake bakes, lending a natural sweetness and moisture that might otherwise be provided by butter, while the firmer Granny Smiths provide a contrasting tartness. McIntosh apples could easily replace the Fujis.

Vegetable oil cooking spray
1 pound Fuji apples (about 2 apples)
8 ounces Granny Smith apples (about 1 apple)
3 tablespoons freshly squeezed lemon juice
1 cup nonfat liquid egg substitute
$1\frac{1}{3}$ cups sugar
2 teaspoons grated lemon zest
$\frac{1}{8}$ teaspoon salt
$2\frac{3}{4}$ cups all-purpose flour
1 tablespoon baking powder

Preheat the oven to 375 degrees. Spray a 9-inch springform pan lightly with the vegetable oil cooking spray and spread the oil evenly over the surface of the pan.

Peel, core, and cut the apples into $\frac{1}{4}$-inch cubes. Put the apple cubes in a glass bowl and toss them with the lemon juice. Set aside.

Combine the egg substitute and sugar in a large bowl and whisk until the sugar has dissolved and the mixture is pale. Mix in the lemon zest and salt. Add the flour and baking powder and mix with a wooden spoon to form a very thick batter. Fold in the apples thoroughly with the wooden spoon.

Scrape the batter into the prepared pan. Bake for about 50 minutes, until the cake is golden and beginning to pull away from the sides of the pan and a tester inserted into the center comes out clean. Cool in the pan for 10 minutes, then remove the sides. Serve warm.

Yield = 12 servings
Fat per serving = 0.46 g.
Calories per serving = 216.8

Torta di Ricotta

Vegetable oil cooking spray
¼ cup fine bread crumbs (see Pantry)
⅔ cup golden raisins
¼ cup golden rum
1 cup sugar
2 tablespoons all-purpose flour
⅛ teaspoon salt

Two 15-ounce containers skim-milk
  ricotta cheese
1½ cups nonfat liquid egg substitute
1 teaspoon grated lemon zest
1 tablespoon grated orange zest
1 tablespoon vanilla extract

THIS CLASSIC cheesecake, made with ricotta (skim-milk ricotta, of course), is lighter and fluffier than the American cream cheese version. It's brimming with golden raisins that have been plumped in rum, and accented with citrus zest. If you use commercial bread crumbs, be sure to select an unseasoned variety.

Preheat the oven to 325 degrees. Spray the inside of a 9-inch springform pan with vegetable oil and dust with the bread crumbs.

Combine the raisins and rum in a small bowl and set aside to soak.

In another small bowl, combine the sugar, flour, and salt.

Put the ricotta cheese in a strainer and shake it to drain any excess moisture. Transfer the cheese to a large mixing bowl. Using an electric mixer at low speed, beat it just enough to break it up. While beating, pour in ½ cup of the egg substitute in a thin stream. Once incorporated, raise the mixer speed to high and slowly add the remaining 1 cup egg substitute. Beat in the sugar mixture. Reduce the speed to low and beat in the citrus zests, vanilla, and the raisins and rum.

Pour the batter into the prepared pan. Bake for about 1 hour and 25 minutes, until the cake is golden and firm to the touch and a tester inserted into the center comes out clean. Allow the cake to cool completely in the pan on a wire rack, 2 to 3 hours, then cover it with aluminum foil and refrigerate it for at least 1 hour or until ready to serve.

Release the springform and cut the cake into 12 thin wedges.

Yield = 12 servings
Fat per serving = 0.20 g.
Calories per serving = 171.4

Jennie's Easter Wheat Pie

This treat is our fat-free rendition of a recipe from Jennie Sama, a legal assistant in our friend Lizanne Ceconi's office. We've tasted several different regional variations of the traditional Easter pie but we like this Neapolitan rendition, with its hint of licorice flavor, the best. Look for hulled, or shelled, wheat in natural or health food stores or Middle Eastern markets. Jennie says the pie is equally good made with rice, wheat germ, or barley in place of the hulled wheat.

½ cup hulled wheat kernels
7 cups water
½ teaspoon salt
½ cup skim milk
1 teaspoon plus 1½ cups sugar
¼ cup finely chopped candied lemon peel
Vegetable oil cooking spray
¼ cup bread crumbs (see Pantry)

1½ pounds skim milk ricotta cheese (about 2⅔ cups)
½ cup nonfat liquid egg substitute
¼ teaspoon ground cinnamon
1 teaspoon vanilla extract
2 tablespoons Anisette (page 254) or Sambuca (page 253)
2 large egg whites, beaten until stiff
Confectioners' sugar for dusting

Combine the wheat kernels and 4 cups of the water in a bowl, cover, and let soak overnight. Using a sieve, strain the wheat and rinse it under cold running water. Place the wheat into a medium nonstick saucepan, along with the salt and the remaining 3 cups water. Bring to a boil over medium-high heat, cover, and reduce the heat to medium-low. Simmer for 1 hour.

Pour off any remaining water that has not been absorbed by the wheat. Add the milk and 1 teaspoon of the sugar to the pan and return the pan to the heat. Bring to a boil over medium-high heat and boil until all the milk has been absorbed, 3 to 5 minutes. Stir in the candied lemon peel and set aside to cool.

Preheat the oven to 350 degrees. Coat a 10-inch glass pie dish lightly with the vegetable oil spray. Put the bread crumbs into the dish, rotating it to coat the bottom and sides evenly and spilling out any crumbs that do not cling to the surface of the dish.

In a large mixing bowl, cream the ricotta and the remaining 1½ cups sugar with an electric mixer at medium speed. Mix in the egg substitute, cinnamon, vanilla, and liqueur. Stir in the wheat mixture. Fold in the egg whites. Pour the batter into the prepared pie dish and place in the center of the oven.

Bake for 1 hour, without opening the oven door. Turn off the oven and allow the pie to cool inside for about 2 hours.

Dust the top of the pie with confectioners' sugar before serving.

Yield = 12 servings
Fat per serving = 0.16 g.
Calories per serving = 159.7

Anise Biscotti

Brittle and just begging to be dunked in a cup of steaming espresso, these biscotti are savory and very grown-up cookies. Take care not to overbake them, since they will continue to harden as they cool.

2¼ cups all-purpose flour
½ tablespoon baking powder
¼ teaspoon salt
1 cup sugar

1 cup nonfat liquid egg substitute
1 tablespoon anise extract
2 teaspoons grated lemon zest

Preheat the oven to 350 degrees. Line a large baking sheet with baker's parchment.

In a large bowl, combine the flour, baking powder, salt, and sugar. Whisk to mix, then make a well in the center of the mixture.

In a small bowl, whisk the egg substitute until frothy. Whisk in the anise and lemon zest. Pour the combination into the well of the flour mixture and stir with a wooden spoon to incorporate the liquid ingredients fully. Gather the dough with lightly floured hands, remove it to a work surface, and divide it in half. Place both halves on the prepared baking sheet and work each piece into a loaf about 10 inches long, 3 inches wide, and ¾ inch high. Bake for about 30 minutes, until golden.

Remove the loaves to the work surface and cut them on the diagonal into ½-inch slices with a serrated knife. Lay the slices flat on the baking sheet. Return them to the oven and toast for about 10 minutes per side, until lightly browned.

Transfer the biscotti to a wire rack to cool.

Yield = About 36 biscotti
Fat per biscotti = 0.06 g.
Calories per biscotti = 49.7

Chocolate Raisin Biscotti

1 cup seedless raisins
¾ cup boiling water
¾ cup nonfat liquid egg substitute
1 cup sugar
1½ tablespoons vanilla extract

2 cups all-purpose flour
⅔ cup Dutch processed cocoa powder
½ tablespoon baking powder
½ teaspoon salt

THE WHOLE FAMILY will enjoy this soft, chewy, chocolaty version of the popular twice-baked (as a loaf, and then after it is sliced) Italian cookie. Don't hesitate to bake a big batch, since biscotti will stay fresh for a week stored in a cookie jar or tin.

Preheat the oven to 350 degrees. Line a large baking sheet with baker's parchment.

In a small bowl, combine the raisins and the boiling water. Set aside to soak for 10 minutes, then drain the raisins.

Meanwhile, combine the egg substitute, sugar, and vanilla in a second bowl. Whisk until the sugar has dissolved and the mixture is frothy, about 1 minute.

In a large mixing bowl, whisk together the flour, cocoa powder, baking powder, and salt. Whisk in the raisins. Make a well in the center and pour in the egg mixture. Stir with a wooden spoon to incorporate the liquid ingredients fully.

Divide the dough in half and place both pieces on the prepared baking sheet. Working with lightly floured hands, form each half into a 9-by-3-inch loaf about ¾ inch high. Bake for about 30 minutes, until well risen and firm to the touch.

Remove the loaves to a work surface and cut ½-inch slices on the diagonal with a serrated knife. Stand the slices upright on the baking sheet and return them to the oven for about 15 minutes more, until very dry to the touch and slightly crisp.

Let the biscotti cool on the sheet on a wire rack.

Yield = About 30 biscotti
Fat per biscotti = 0.27 g.
Calories per biscotti = 70.7

Liqueurs

(Spiriti)

Blackberry Grappa 〜 Pear Grappa 〜 Honey-Peach Grappa 〜 Sambuca 〜 Anisette 〜 Hazelnut Liqueur 〜 Limoncello Sorrento Style 〜 Amaretto Pronto

16. *Liqueurs*

(Spiriti)

Perhaps liqueurs are not as popular as wine, but Italians do enjoy them. In particular, grappa, the fiery brandy extracted from the skins of pressed grapes, is a national ritual. Flavored or straight, simply served or elaborately bottled, grappa is everything from a digestive aid to the "correction" in *caffè corretto*. To be perfectly honest, we prefer the fire tempered with a bit of flavoring—an easy enough process. Hence the recipes for various fruit infusions that follow.

We also make two licorice-flavored concoctions, a clear sambuca, like the cordial usually seen sporting coffee beans, and a reddish brown anisette of the sort often splashed into a cup of espresso. Rounding out the after-dinner offerings are Limoncello, a robust lemon cordial, along with hazelnut- and almond-flavored liqueurs, all made from a vodka base.

The grappa infusions simply involve combining the fruit with the brandy, mustering the patience to let it steep for 6 to 8 weeks in a cool, dry place, and straining. Some of the vodka infusions involve two steps, although the steeping time is shorter in most cases. Fruit, nuts, or flavorings are steeped in vodka, strained, and then combined with a sugar syrup. The easiest cordial to make is an amaretto, which is ready to drink in less than 2 hours.

The ideal places to steep cordials are in a pantry or kitchen cabinet, away from direct sunlight and any heat source. Don't steep them in the refrigerator, and do start with a high-quality liquor.

Blackberry Grappa

GRAPPA, A STRONG spirit made from the distilled pulp of wine grapes, is an ideal medium for infusing flavors. Know before you start that grappa can range from very basic to reasonably refined these days; you get what you pay for. The better the grappa you start with, the better your flavored cordial will be.

1 pint blackberries, picked over

Two strips orange peel (each about 1 by 3 inches, pith removed)

4 cloves

2 tablespoons sugar

2 cups grappa

Put the blackberries, orange peel, cloves, and sugar in a 1-quart container. Top with the grappa. Cover and store in a cupboard or pantry for 6 weeks. Strain through a fine-mesh sieve lined with a damp coffee filter, then set aside for 2 more days before serving.

If you wish, add a few fresh blackberries to each serving glass.

Yield = 2 cups, or 16 ounces
Fat per ounce = 0.11 g.
Calories per ounce = 84.8

Pear Grappa

14 to 16 ounces Anjou pears (about 2 pears), cored and diced (2½ to 2¾ cups)

3 tablespoons sugar

2 cups grappa

In a 1-quart container, combine the pears, sugar, and grappa. Seal and shake. Set aside in a cupboard or pantry for 2 months to steep. Strain through a fine-mesh sieve and discard the pears.

The grappa is ready to serve immediately.

Yield = 2 cups, or 16 ounces
Fat per ounce = 0.11 g.
Calories per ounce = 89.1

You DON'T NEED A basement still to create your own cordials, just brandy or vodka and a common pantry flavoring or two. In this case, fruit and sugar are allowed to steep in grappa, a robust Italian brandy, for about 2 months. Tuck the mixture in a cool, dark place, away from sunlight and heat, but don't refrigerate it.

Honey-Peach Grappa

¼ cup clover honey

1½ pounds peaches (about 4 peaches), peeled, pitted, and chopped (about 3 cups)

2 cups grappa

Put the honey in a small, microwave-safe container and microwave at full power just long enough so that it is liquid but not hot, about 20 seconds. (You can also liquefy the honey by heating it in a small saucepan over very low heat for a minute or two, taking care not to bring it to a boil.)

Combine the honey with the peaches and grappa in a 1-quart container. Seal, shake, and steep in a cupboard or pantry for 6 weeks. Strain through a fine-mesh sieve, cover again, and steep for about 1 week more.

Strain again through a sieve lined with a damp coffee filter or a double thickness of cheesecloth, allowing the grappa to drip through slowly. (This could take 1 to 2 hours.)

Yield = 2 cups, or 16 ounces
Fat per ounce = 0.03 g.
Calories per ounce = 93.9

Sambuca

3 cups water

3 cups sugar

½ cup vodka

¼ cup anise extract

Combine the water and sugar in a medium saucepan over medium-high heat. Bring to a full boil, stirring until the sugar dissolves and turns clear. Boil for 10 minutes, then remove from the heat and cool completely. Stir in the vodka. Stir in the anise (which will turn the mixture cloudy). Transfer the mixture to a 1-quart container, cover, and set aside in a cupboard or pantry for 7 to 10 days, until it turns clear again.

Yield = 4 cups, or 32 ounces
Fat per ounce = 0 g.
Calories per ounce = 84.1

THIS LICORICE-flavored liqueur, particularly identified with Rome, is usually served straight up in a pony glass with three coffee beans floating on top. Made from the fruit of the elder bush, sambuca is somewhat sweet and syrupy.

Anisette

Made with licorice-tasting anise, which has long been considered a digestive aid, anisette has a faint lemony undertone. The cordial can be either reddish brown, as our version is, or clear. We add a bit of glycerin (available at most pharmacies), which thickens and lends a nice feel on the tongue. Anisette is often added to espresso.

2 tablespoons aniseed

2 cups vodka

1/2 teaspoon grated lemon zest

1/4 cup water

1/2 cup sugar

1 teaspoon glycerin

Arrange the aniseed on a work surface between sheets of wax paper and crush it with a rolling pin or other heavy object. Combine the crushed seed in a 1-pint container with the vodka and lemon zest. Seal and shake. Store in a cupboard or pantry for about 6 weeks, shaking periodically.

Strain the liquid through a fine-mesh sieve lined with a damp coffee filter.

In a small saucepan, bring the water and sugar to a boil over medium heat, stirring until the sugar dissolves completely. Boil for about 3 minutes to create a thick, clear syrup. Remove the syrup from the heat and cool completely. Transfer the cooled syrup to the 1-quart container with the strained vodka mixture and add the glycerin. Seal and shake. The liqueur will be ready to serve in 3 to 4 days.

Yield = 2 cups, or 16 ounces
Fat per ounce = 0.14 g.
Calories per ounce = 91.9

Hazelnut Liqueur

1 pound hazelnuts, shelled and
   coarsely chopped (1⅓ to 1½ cups)
2 cups vodka
½ vanilla bean

½ cup sugar
¼ cup water
½ teaspoon glycerin (available at
   most pharmacies)

Combine the nuts, vodka, and vanilla bean in a 1-quart container. Seal and shake. Store in a cupboard or pantry for 10 days.

Strain the liquid twice through a fine-mesh sieve; the second time, line the sieve with a damp coffee filter.

In a small saucepan, combine the sugar and water. Bring to a boil over low heat, stirring until the sugar dissolves. Continue to boil for about 2 minutes, until a clear syrup forms. Remove the syrup from the heat and cool it to room temperature.

In a 1-pint container, combine the syrup and the strained vodka mixture. Add the glycerin, seal, and shake again. The liqueur should be ready to drink in 2 to 3 days.

Yield = 2 cups, or 16 ounces
Fat per ounce = 0.30 g.
Calories per ounce = 353.5

TASTING LIKE LIQUID filberts, this liqueur is equally good served straight up as a cordial, used in a variety of baked goods, or drizzled over gelato or custard. As is the case in all liqueur preparations, take care to let the sugar syrup cool completely before combining it with the steeped vodka, so as not to burn off the alcohol.

Limoncello Sorrento Style

4 lemons

2 cups plus 2 tablespoons 100-proof vodka

1 cup sugar

1¼ cups water

1 tablespoon freshly squeezed lemon juice

Peel the lemons, taking care to remove all the pith. In a 1-pint container, combine the lemon peel and 1 cup of the vodka. Seal and store in a cabinet or pantry for 1 month.

Combine the sugar and water in a small saucepan. Bring to a full boil over high heat, stirring until the sugar dissolves. Boil for 3 minutes. Remove from the heat and cool completely, then stir in the lemon juice, the remaining 1 cup plus 2 tablespoons vodka, and the steeped vodka mixture. Transfer the liqueur to a 1-quart container, seal, and steep for 1 month more.

Strain through a fine-mesh sieve. The limoncello is ready to serve immediately. Store it in the freezer.

Yield = 4 cups, or 32 ounces
Fat per ounce = 0 g.
Calories per ounce = 68.3

Amaretto Pronto

4 cups water

2 cups sugar

¼ cup dark corn syrup

2 tablespoons plus 2 teaspoons
  almond extract

1 tablespoon vanilla extract

¾ cup vodka

Combine the water and sugar in a large saucepan. Bring to a full boil over high heat, stirring until the sugar dissolves. Boil for 20 minutes. Remove from the heat, stir in the corn syrup, and allow the mixture to cool for about 1 hour. Stir in the almond and vanilla extracts and the vodka.

The amaretto is ready to drink immediately.

Yield = 4 cups, or 32 ounces
Fat per ounce = 0 g.
Calories per ounce = 74.4

PERHAPS ATTESTING to amaretto's worldwide popularity, this recipe is adapted from one we received not from an elderly couple in Saronno but from our friends Deborah and Jim Hendricks in Duck, North Carolina, who end their recipe by saying "Bottle and enjoy!"

Amaretto is often made using apricot pits. In the past, we've made a version by steeping almonds in vodka, but it's a bit involved and takes almost 2 weeks to age—much too long for Deb and Jim. Their quick version, made with almond extract, is ready in less than 2 hours.

Source Guide

BAKER'S CATALOGUE
P.O. Box 876
Norwich, VT 05055
800-827-6836
Flours, polenta, bakeware

BALDUCCI'S
Shop-at-Home Service
42-26 13th Street
Long Island City, NY 11101
800-225-3822
A broad range of high-quality Italian foods

W. ATLEE BURPEE & CO.
300 Park Avenue
Warminster, PA 18991
800-888-1447
http://www.burpee.com
Arugula, radicchio, and assorted herb seeds

CHEF'S CATALOG
3215 Commercial Avenue
Northbrook, IL 60062
800-338-3232
Pasta- and pizza-making supplies, gelato makers, and assorted kitchenware

CONVITO ITALIANO
1515 Sheridan Road
Wilmette, IL 60091
847-251-3654
A broad range of high-quality Italian foods

CORTI BROTHERS
5810 Folsom Boulevard
Sacramento, CA 95819
800-509-3663
A broad range of high-quality Italian foods

DEAN & DELUCA
560 Broadway
New York, NY 10012
800-221-7714
A broad range of high-quality Italian foods;
dried beans and mushrooms

KITCHEN GLAMOUR
39049 Webb Court
Westland, MI 48185
800-641-1252
Pasta-making supplies, including
ravioli molds

MANGANARO FOODS
488 Ninth Avenue
New York, NY 10018
800-472-5264
A broad range of high-quality
Italian foods

NEW YORK CAKE & BAKING DISTRIBUTOR
56 West 22nd Street
New York, NY 10010
800-94-CAKE-9
Bakeware, including panettone molds

RIVER VALLEY RANCH
P.O. Box 898
New Munster, WI 53152
800-SHROOMS
Mushroom-growing kits

SHEPHERD'S GARDEN SEEDS
30 Irene Street
Torrington, CT 06790
860-482-3638
http://www.shepherdseeds.com
A large assortment of arugula, radicchio, frisée, dandelion, and
cipolline seeds; assorted herb plants and seeds; sea salt

LEONARD SOLOMON WINES & SPIRITS
1456 North Dayton
Chicago, IL 60622
312-915-5911
http://www.winecheese.com
High-quality wines and Italian specialty foods, including cheeses
and Vialone Nano, Carnaroli, and Cal Riso rice

SPICELAND, INC.
P.O. Box 34378
Chicago, IL 60634
800-FLAVOR-1
A broad range of high-quality herbs, spices, and seeds; sea salt;
vanilla, anise, and almond extracts

SUR LA TABLE
84 Pine Street
Seattle, WA 98101
800-240-0853
Pizza-making and bread-baking supplies

WILLIAMS-SONOMA
Mail-Order Dept.
   P.O. Box 7456
   San Francisco, CA 94120
   800-541-2233
   Assorted kitchenware and bakeware, including olive oil sprayers,
   removable-bottom tart pans, springform pans, mandolines

ZABAR'S
Mail-Order Catalog
   2245 Broadway
   New York, NY 10024
   800-221-3347
   A broad range of high-quality Italian foods; assorted kitchenware
   and bakeware

ZINGERMAN'S
   422 Detroit Street
   Ann Arbor, MI 48104
   888-363-8162
   High-quality oils and vinegars

Index

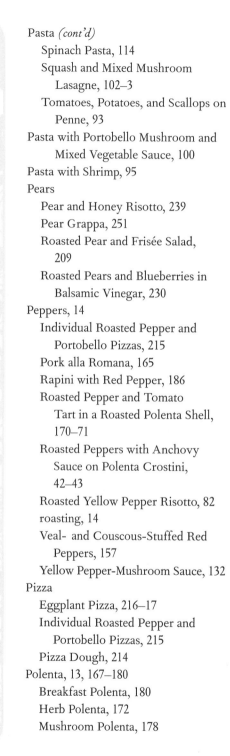